100 Questions (and Answers)
About Research Ethics

Q&A SAGE 100 Questions and Answers Series

Neil J. Salkind, Series Editor

1. *100 Questions (and Answers) About Research Methods*, by Neil J. Salkind

2. *100 Questions (and Answers) About Tests and Measurement*, by Bruce B. Frey

3. *100 Questions (and Answers) About Statistics*, by Neil J. Salkind

4. *100 Questions (and Answers) About Qualitative Research* by Lisa M. Given

5. *100 Questions (and Answers) About Research Ethics* by Emily E. Anderson and Amy Corneli

Visit **sagepub.com/100qa** for a current listing of titles in this series.

100 Questions (and Answers) About Research Ethics

Emily E. Anderson
Loyola University Chicago

Amy Corneli
Duke University

Los Angeles | London | New Delhi
Singapore | Washington DC | Melbourne

FOR INFORMATION:

SAGE Publications, Inc.
2455 Teller Road
Thousand Oaks, California 91320
E-mail: order@sagepub.com

SAGE Publications Ltd.
1 Oliver's Yard
55 City Road
London EC1Y 1SP
United Kingdom

SAGE Publications India Pvt. Ltd.
B 1/I 1 Mohan Cooperative Industrial Area
Mathura Road, New Delhi 110 044
India

SAGE Publications Asia-Pacific Pte. Ltd.
3 Church Street
#10-04 Samsung Hub
Singapore 049483

Printed in the United States of America

Library of Congress Cataloging-in-Publication Data

Names: Anderson, Emily E., author. | Corneli, Amy, author.

Title: 100 questions (and answers) about research ethics / Emily E. Anderson, Loyola University, Chicago, Amy Corneli, Duke University.

Other titles: One hundred questions (and answers) about research ethics

Description: Thousand Oaks, CA : SAGE, [2018] | Includes bibliographical references and index.

Identifiers: LCCN 2017043148 | ISBN 9781506348704 (pbk. : alk. paper)

Subjects: LCSH: Social sciences—Research—Moral and ethical aspects. | Research—Moral and ethical aspects. | Participant observation—Moral and ethical aspects.

Classification: LCC H62 .A5895 2018 | DDC 174/.90014—dc23 LC record available at https://lccn.loc.gov/2017043148

This book is printed on acid-free paper.

Acquisitions Editor: Helen Salmon
Editorial Assistant: Chelsea Neve
Production Editor: Christine Dahlin
Copy Editor: Ellen Howard
Typesetter: C&M Digitals (P) Ltd.
Proofreader: Alison Syring
Indexer: Amy Murphy
Cover Designer: Candice Harman
Marketing Manager: Susannah Goldes

17 18 19 20 21 10 9 8 7 6 5 4 3 2 1

Contents

Preface   **xi**

Acknowledgments   **xiii**

About the Authors   **xv**

**PART 1: UNDERSTANDING ETHICS IN
RESEARCH WITH HUMAN PARTICIPANTS**   **1**

1. What Is Ethics, and How Does It Apply to
Research With Human Participants?   2

2. What Is the Ethical Justification for Conducting
Research With Human Participants?   4

3. What Broad Ethical Principles Apply to
Research With Human Participants?   5

4. What Ethical Guidance and Regulations
Inform Research With Human Participants, and
What, If Anything, Has Changed Over Time?   6

5. What Is the Relationship Between Ethics and Compliance?   8

6. What Are the Potential Consequences of Ignoring
Ethical Principles and Regulations?   9

7. What Kinds of Research Are Considered Unethical, and
What Are Some Examples of Serious Ethical Lapses in
Social and Behavioral Sciences Research?   11

8. How Do Standard Ethical Practices for Research Vary Among
Academic Disciplines in the Social and Behavioral Sciences?   14

9. Who Is Responsible for Ensuring Research
Is Conducted Ethically?   15

10. When I Begin Developing My Research,
What Ethical Issues Should I First Consider?   17

PART 2: ASSESSING RESEARCH RISKS AND BENEFITS   **19**

11. What Is Risk, and What Are the Risks in Social and
Behavioral Sciences Research?   20

12. How Do I Identify Risks in My Research—and Minimize Them?   22

13. What Is Meant by "Minimal Risk"?   24

14. What Are the Potential Benefits of Research?   25

15. How Do I Design My Research So That the Risk–Benefit Balance Is Favorable?   27

16. How Do I Make Sure That Participants in My Research Do Not Overestimate the Benefits or Underestimate the Risks?   28

17. I Will Conduct Research on a Sensitive Topic. What Should I Do to Prevent Psychological Harms?   30

PART 3: PROTECTING PRIVACY AND CONFIDENTIALITY   33

18. What Is Meant by "Privacy" and "Confidentiality," and Is There a Difference?   34

19. What Makes Data De-Identified?   35

20. What Makes Data Anonymous?   37

21. When Is Information (or Behavior) Considered Private Rather Than Public, and How Can Private Information Be Used in Research?   39

22. What Can I Do to Protect Participants' Privacy During Data Collection and Reporting?   41

23. What Can I Do to Protect the Confidentiality of Information Collected?   42

24. When Must I Share Study Data—and Participant Names—With Individuals Outside of the Research Team?   44

25. What Is a Certificate of Confidentiality?   46

26. What Privacy Laws Must I Follow?   47

PART 4: PROTECTING VULNERABLE POPULATIONS   49

27. What Kinds of Participants Are Considered Vulnerable in Research, and What Are Some Ways to Protect Vulnerable Participants?   50

28. What Ethical Issues Should I Consider When Conducting Research With Prisoners?   54

29. What Ethical Issues Should I Consider When Conducting Research With Pregnant Women?   57

30. What Ethical Issues Should I Consider When Conducting Research With Children?   59

31. What Ethical Issues Should I Consider When Conducting Research With Individuals Who Have Experienced Traumatic Events?   61

32. What Ethical Issues Should I Consider
When Conducting Research With Adults Who May Lack
Decision-Making Capacity Due to Cognitive Impairment?   63

33. What Ethical Issues Should I Consider When Conducting
Research With Students, Particularly Students Whom I Teach?   65

PART 5: OBTAINING INFORMED CONSENT   **67**

34. What Is Informed Consent?   68

35. What Is the Informed Consent Process?   69

36. What Is an Informed Consent Form?   71

37. When Is Informed Consent Required?   72

38. What Is the Difference Between Written and Verbal Informed
Consent, and When Can Verbal Informed Consent Be Used?   74

39. What Are the Requirements for Informing
Participants in Research That Is Determined to Be
Exempt From the Federal Regulations?   76

40. What Type of Information Must Be Included in an
Informed Consent Form?   77

41. How Do I Write a Consent Form That Is Easy to Understand?   80

42. How Do I Obtain Informed Consent?   81

43. Who Can Consent to Research Participation?   83

44. What Do I Do With the Consent Form After It Is
Signed by a Participant?   84

45. How Do I Obtain Informed Consent From a Prospective
Participant Who Cannot Read the Consent Form?   85

46. How Do I Obtain Informed Consent From Prospective
Participants Who Speak a Different Language From Mine?   87

47. How Can I Obtain Informed Consent From Individuals
With Cognitive Impairments or Developmental Disabilities?   89

48. How Do I Know If a Prospective Participant
Understands the Research?   91

49. How Do I Ensure That a Participant's Consent Is Voluntary?   93

50. Do I Need to Obtain Informed Consent Before
Asking Screening Questions?   95

51. Do I Need to Obtain Informed Consent
From Individuals to Use Their Existing Data
That Were Collected for Other Purposes?   96

52. How Are Parents Involved in Decision Making
    About Their Children's Participation in Research? 98

53. What Type of Agreement Do I Need From
    Children So They Can Participate in Research? 100

54. How Should I Obtain Informed Consent From
    Prospective Participants When I'm Conducting
    Research Outside the United States? 102

PART 6: DESIGNING ETHICAL RESEARCH **105**

55. How Do I Ensure That Eligibility Criteria
    Are Appropriate and Fair? 106

56. What Strategies Can I Use to Ethically Recruit
    People to Join My Research? 107

57. When Is It Appropriate to Pay Participants for
    Taking Part in Research? 110

58. How Do I Determine the Appropriate Amount to
    Pay Research Participants? 112

59. What Ethical Issues Should I Consider
    When Conducting Focus Group Discussions? 113

60. What Ethical Issues Should I Consider
    When Conducting Participant Observations? 115

61. What Are Some of the Ethical Issues Raised by
    Deception in Research, and When Is It Ethically
    Acceptable to Use Deception? 117

62. What Ethical Issues Should I Consider If
    My Intervention Research Includes a Control Group? 119

63. What Ethical Issues Should I Consider
    When Conducting Research in a Defined Community? 121

64. What Is the Relationship Between Community
    Engagement and Research Ethics? 123

65. What Does Cultural Competence Mean, and
    How Do I Apply It to Research Ethics? 126

66. What Ethical Guidelines and Regulations Should I
    Consider When Conducting Research in Another Country? 128

**PART 7: ADDRESSING ETHICAL ISSUES IN
    ONLINE RESEARCH** **129**

67. Are There Specific Ethical Guidelines for Conducting
    Research Online? 130

68. What Ethical Issues Should I Consider
When Recruiting Study Participants Online? 131

69. What Ethical Issues Should I Consider
When Collecting *New* Data Online? 133

70. What Ethical Issues Should I Consider
When Using Data That Already *Exist* Online? 135

71. How Do I Document Informed Consent
When Conducting Research Online—and
Ensure That Participants Understand the Research? 137

72. Is It Ethical for Me to Join an Online Discussion Group or
Chat Room for Research Purposes Without Informing
the Group That I'm a Researcher? 139

73. How Do I Verify the Age of Individuals
Who Participate in My Online Research? 141

PART 8: NEGOTIATING THE IRB REVIEW PROCESS **143**

74. What Is an IRB, and Who Are the Members? 144

75. How Do I Know If My Study Must Be Reviewed by an IRB? 146

76. How Do I Know Which IRB—and How Many IRBs—Must
Review and Approve My Proposed Research? 148

77. When Is a Research Study "Exempt" From the
Federal Research Regulations, and What Does This Mean? 149

78. What Is Expedited Review? 151

79. What Is the Difference Between Expedited and
Full Board Review? 152

80. What Materials Will I Need to Submit to the IRB? 153

81. What Can I Expect During the IRB Review Process? 155

82. Before IRB Approval, What Can I Do and Not Do? 156

83. What Are Changes That the IRB Can Request, and
How Do I Respond? 158

84. What Should I Do If I Want to Change the Protocol,
Consent Form, or Other Documents After They Have Been
Approved by an IRB? 160

85. What Should I Do If My Research Requires Continuing Review? 162

86. I Am Collecting Data for a Class Project. Do I Need IRB Approval? 164

87. I Am Conducting an Evaluation of a Program.
Do I Need IRB Approval? 165

**PART 9: UNDERSTANDING ETHICAL
RESPONSIBILITIES OF DATA USE**   **167**

88. What Confidentiality Procedures Should I Put in Place
    After All Data Have Been Collected?   168

89. How Long Must I Keep My Research Records?   169

90. When Can I Destroy My Research Files?   171

91. Do I Have an Ethical Obligation to Publish
    My Research Findings?   173

92. Can I Publish My Findings If I Did Not Get IRB Approval or
    Obtain Informed Consent From Participants?   174

93. What Do I Need to Do to Ensure That I Protect
    Participants' Identities When Sharing Datasets With Others and
    That Participants Are Informed of This Possibility? 175

94. Can I Show Participants Their Transcripts or the
    Transcripts of Other Participants?   177

95. Should I Share the Results of My Research
    With Study Participants?   179

**PART 10: HANDLING ETHICAL ISSUES THAT
ARISE DURING RESEARCH IMPLEMENTATION**   **181**

96. What Should I Do If I—or a Study Staff Member or
    Participant—Do Something That Was Not in
    the Approved Protocol?   182

97. What Should I Do If Someone Is Physically, Emotionally, or
    Socially Harmed From Taking Part in My Research?   184

98. What Should I Do If a Participant Says He Wants to
    Harm Himself or Someone Else?   185

99. What Should I Do If I Lose My Field Notes or
    Other Hard Copies of Data?   186

100. What Should I Do If a Participant Says a
     Person's Name or the Name of an Organization
     During an Interview or Focus Group Discussion?   187

References and Resources   **189**

Index   **197**

Preface

Researchers in the social and behavioral sciences must follow recognized ethical standards and federal research regulations when they conduct their research. However, it is often challenging to determine appropriate actions in a given research study. In part, this is because standards, regulations, and other forms of guidance were initially developed with medical research as the model. Interpreting what this guidance means for an ethnographic study, a longitudinal behavioral survey, or a study of a behavioral intervention, for example, is not always straightforward. Guidance is general, and each study is unique in its combination of research question, approach, methods, study population, and research team. Additionally, many graduate programs do not have the resources to offer more than a few lectures related to research ethics, which means that students do not have opportunities to learn the reasoning needed to guide ethical decision making in real-world situations. Often, questions remain among researchers on how to apply ethical standards when developing and implementing social and behavioral research.

100 Questions (and Answers) About Research Ethics identifies and answers essential questions on the ethical guidelines and regulations that govern human subjects research, while focusing specifically on how these standards are applied to research in the social and behavioral sciences. *100 Questions (and Answers) About Research Ethics* can serve as an ancillary text for a variety of undergraduate and graduate research methods courses. It is also a useful resource for students developing their thesis and dissertation proposals, for faculty designing research, and for members of institutional review boards (IRBs) that review social and behavioral sciences research.

The questions are divided into 10 parts:

- Part 1: Understanding Ethics in Research With Human Participants
- Part 2: Assessing Research Risks and Benefits
- Part 3: Protecting Privacy and Confidentiality
- Part 4: Protecting Vulnerable Populations
- Part 5: Obtaining Informed Consent
- Part 6: Designing Ethical Research
- Part 7: Addressing Ethical Issues in Online Research

- Part 8: Negotiating the IRB Review Process
- Part 9: Understanding Ethical Responsibilities of Data Use
- Part 10: Handling Ethical Issues That Arise During Research Implementation

This book can be read cover to cover, or specific questions can be consulted as issues arise. Although each question is intended to stand alone, there are many areas of overlap, as research is not a linear process. Our intention is for this book to be a handy resource, but we cannot cover everything in this short volume. Therefore, we have provided both a list of related questions at the end of each individual question and a section of References and Resources at the end of the book.

A few notes on what is *not* covered in this short book. We do not have sufficient space to delve into the rich expanse of philosophical and ethical theory that underpins the guiding principles for human research. Nor do we cover topics related to research integrity and misconduct, such as plagiarism, data falsification, or authorship. We focus specifically on the ethics of conducting research with human beings.

A revision to the federal research regulations (Federal Policy for the Protection of Human Subjects, Text of the Final Common Rule, Part 46, Subpart A, Protection of Human Subjects) was published in the Federal Register (Vol. 82, No. 12) on Thursday, January 19, 2017 (https://www .federalregister.gov/documents/2017/01/19/2017-01058/federal-policy-for -the-protection-of-human-subjects). The final version will be codified at 45 C.F.R. §. 46, Subpart A, on January 19, 2018, soon after this book is published. We reference the new research regulations throughout the book; however, because we wrote the book before the final regulations were published, we used information from the Federal Register when referencing Subpart A of the federal research regulations. Because the Common Rule was revised in January 2017, with changes to go into effect in January 2018, specific guidance from the Office for Human Research Protections (https://www.hhs.gov/ohrp/) will continue to emerge to assist researchers and IRBs in interpreting and applying these revisions.

While we frequently refer to the federal regulations for research (45 C.F.R. § 46, the Common Rule), we want to emphasize that different institutions may have additional policies, and different disciplines have additional standards of practices. We also want to emphasize that following the regulations—compliance—is the *minimum* for ethical research. We hope the guidance we provide in this volume encourages researchers to be thoughtful in their approaches and strive not only to protect research participants from harm but to treat them with optimal respect and care.

Acknowledgments

SAGE and the authors gratefully acknowledge feedback from the following reviewers:

Wayne A. Babchuk, University of Nebraska–Lincoln

Marilyn Bruin, University of Minnesota

Elizabeth Buchanan, University of Wisconsin–Stout

Robert L. Dahlgren, SUNY Fredonia

Todd M. Freeberg, The University of Tennessee–Knoxville

Debra Osnowitz, Clark University

Dena Plemmons, University of California, Riverside

Kenneth A. Richman, MCPHS University

Artineh Samkian, University of Southern California

Carla J. Thompson, University of West Florida

About the Authors

Emily E. Anderson, PhD, MPH, is an associate professor in the Neiswanger Institute for Bioethics at Loyola University Chicago, Stritch School of Medicine. She teaches courses in research ethics, responsible conduct of research, and empirical bioethics research to a variety of graduate and medical students. Her areas of interest include ethical issues in research with special populations; ethical issues in public health and health disparities research; and the application of qualitative research techniques to the study of research ethics. Dr. Anderson has published articles in numerous bioethics journals, presented at national conferences, and serves in several editorial positions. She has over ten years of experience serving on six different IRBs.

Amy Corneli, PhD, MPH, is an associate professor in the Department of Population Health Sciences in the School of Medicine at Duke University. She is also a Faculty Associate in the Trent Center for Bioethics, Humanities, and History of Medicine, and faculty member in the Duke Clinical Research Institute. A social scientist by training, Dr. Corneli has conducted research in health, primarily biomedical HIV prevention, and bioethics in multiple countries in sub-Saharan Africa, the Middle East, South and Southeast Asia, and North America. Her bioethics research has focused on innovative methods for improving informed consent comprehension and shortening consent forms, acceptability of informed assent, and functioning of research ethics committees. Dr. Corneli has also been involved in IRB capacity-building activities in sub-Saharan Africa and serves as an associate editor for a bioethics journal.

Sara Miller McCune founded SAGE Publishing in 1965 to support the dissemination of usable knowledge and educate a global community. SAGE publishes more than 1000 journals and over 800 new books each year, spanning a wide range of subject areas. Our growing selection of library products includes archives, data, case studies and video. SAGE remains majority owned by our founder and after her lifetime will become owned by a charitable trust that secures the company's continued independence.

Los Angeles | London | New Delhi | Singapore | Washington DC | Melbourne

PART 1

UNDERSTANDING ETHICS IN RESEARCH WITH HUMAN PARTICIPANTS

What Is Ethics, and How Does It Apply to Research With Human Participants?

"Ethics" refers to the study of what *ought* to (or ought not to) be done. The term also describes a collective body of guidance regarding questions of good or right action. Ethical decision making is the process of identifying, evaluating, and choosing among options regarding a problem that has an ethical dimension. What kinds of problems have ethical dimensions? Those that involve and may impact humans.

Research, or the scientific study of human beings and their behavior, began centuries before there were any formal rules or codes of research ethics written down on paper. However, since ancient times, scholars in philosophy and religion have articulated guiding principles regarding how humans should treat each other. Arguably, there is a fair amount of agreement regarding such treatment, perhaps best evidenced by the Golden Rule: "Do unto others as you would have them do unto you." Rooted in the Judeo-Christian traditions, this "common morality" is the foundation for codes of ethics for research developed by professional societies like the American Psychological Association as well as the federal research regulations. Research ethics codes and regulations interpret and apply the common morality for the research context by following three key principles: respect for persons, beneficence, and justice. More on these principles throughout the rest of the book.

Research ethics is a form of applied ethics: that is, the study of and rules for what ought to be done in the specific context of research. During the past 50 years, research ethics has developed as a specialized area of study to determine the best courses of action for scientists who conduct research, and in particular, research with humans. Such scholarly analysis has become essential as research with human participants becomes more specialized, complex, and multi- and interdisciplinary. The study of research ethics is devoted to identifying the standards to which researchers should be held, including the parameters that should guide researcher behavior and the practices and processes that best protect human research participants within specific contexts. Such parameters, practices, and processes are articulated in federal research regulations; professional codes of ethics; institutional policies; and various other forms of guidance such as white papers, government reports, reports from nongovernmental organizations, and research ethics scholarship. This book aims to explain in 100 questions and answers the general ethical rules for social and behavioral research with human participants.

More questions? See #2, #5, and #10.

What Is the Ethical Justification for Conducting Research With Human Participants?

Although research involving humans began centuries ago, the best known, most often cited ethical justification for including humans in research was first fully articulated by Hans Jonas in his seminal 1969 article, "Philosophical Reflections on Experimenting With Human Subjects." As described by Jonas, there is an innate human curiosity that drives us to learn more about ourselves and our environment. This desire leads us to conduct research through observation and experimental techniques, not only for the sake of knowledge but also with the ultimate goal of improving the human condition and our planet. As a society, we need research with human participants to learn more about ourselves; learning more about how humans behave and interact is necessary to improve the human condition. Therefore, including humans in research is justified by the potential for the common or collective good. However, all research requires the balance of two important goals: protecting participants from exploitation and harm, and providing equal access to the direct and indirect benefits of research. Ideally, all will benefit from discoveries made by research. Research with humans poses a tension between individual welfare and the common good. Therefore, parameters must be set on research practices. Determining and articulating these limits is the focus of research ethics scholarship and the aim of professional ethics codes and federal research regulations.

More questions? See #3, #8, and #10.

What Broad Ethical Principles Apply to Research With Human Participants?

The ethical framework that underpins the federal research regulations as well as most professional codes of research ethics does not privilege any one ethical theory or approach but rather articulates a set of overall principles: respect for persons, beneficence, and justice. These principles are outlined in the *Belmont Report* (1979), a key U.S. research ethics document. The principle of respect for persons demands that individuals control what happens to them. Beneficent research promotes good and avoids harm. Justice requires fairness in the selection of research participants. It also requires an equitable distribution of the benefits and burdens of research so that no one group disproportionately bears the burden or receives the benefits of research.

These three principles must be balanced in all research with human participants. For example, sometimes risks must be taken in order to attain the potential benefits. However, there is no hard-and-fast rule regarding the appropriate weighting of principles in specific situations. Reasonable people may disagree about how best to weigh the risks and benefits of a particular research study based on whether they prioritize respect for persons or beneficence. This is arguably both a strength and a weakness of the Belmont research ethics framework.

More questions? See #4, #7, and #10.

What Ethical Guidance and Regulations Inform Research With Human Participants, and What, If Anything, Has Changed Over Time?

For many centuries, research and researchers' behavior was not systematically regulated by any laws. Although informal standards of conduct existed within certain circles, until quite recently, there were no normative rules or formal mechanisms for guiding, monitoring, or enforcing ethical scientific behavior, or for punishing those who engaged in behavior that we would now consider unethical. In the early 20th century, the first professional codes of ethics, primarily targeting medical researchers, were written in response to the discovery of—and public outrage over—significant harms to research participants. These include the Nuremberg Code, written in 1947 after Nazi doctors were tried in a court of law and found guilty of conducting harmful experiments on prisoners in concentration camps; and the Declaration of Helsinki (2013), first issued by the World Medical Association in 1964, which expanded on the principles outlined in the Nuremberg Code and linked them to the responsibilities of physicians who conduct research. Although at the time they were developed these codes reflected basic, agreed-on best practices for research involving human participants, they were not (and still are not) enforceable.

Ultimately, as more instances of disrespect and abuse of human research participants became known, the American public demanded that the federal government step in and do something. In 1974, President Nixon established the National Commission for the Protection of Human Subjects of Biomedical and Behavioral Research. This was in response to a national news story about a government-funded study in Tuskegee, Alabama. Hundreds of Black men with syphilis were followed for decades; but they were neither told they had the disease nor treated, despite the availability of affordable and effective medication. In 1979, the National Commission issued the *Belmont Report*, which details the three foundational principles for ethical research—respect for persons, beneficence, and justice.

Now, all research funded by the U.S. government must follow federal regulations that were subsequently developed based on these principles. These regulations are published in the *Code of Federal Regulations* (CFR), which contains all rules and regulations issued by the U.S. government. Several of the CFR's 50 sections (called "titles") include subsections relevant to the conduct of research with human participants, such as Title 45 Public Welfare, Part 46 Protection of Human Subjects (issued by the Department of Health and Human Services [DHHS]). Although not mandated by the U.S. government, some academic and other research institutions extend these rules to all research conducted by their employees and students, regardless of funding source.

Federal guidance is regularly reviewed and updated. In January 2017, revisions to 45 C.F.R. § 46 were published by the Office of Human Research Protections (OHRP), the DHHS office responsible for the oversight of human research (http://www.hhs.gov/ohrp/). Title 45 C.F.R. § 46 defines "research" and "human subject." It also outlines ethical criteria for research conducted with human participants, such as the information that must be told to participants about the research so they can make an informed decision about participation; and the structure, function, and registration of institutional review boards.

More questions? See #3, #8, and #9.

What Is the Relationship Between Ethics and Compliance?

Ethics requires thoughtful consideration of the range of possible options in a given situation. For a researcher, ethics also requires a professional commitment to put the safety and well-being of research participants and their communities first, and to strive always to maximize benefits and minimize harm in research activities. To be ethical or to make an ethical (good) decision is to consider the viewpoints of and potential outcomes for all affected stakeholders—including participants, researchers, and the general public as future beneficiaries of the research. Ethical researchers aim to make decisions that are good for everyone involved in the research but that are first and foremost good for participants.

Compliance refers to following the rules. As a researcher, it is necessary, but not sufficient, to know and follow the rules. When it comes to determining what is right and wrong in research, compliance with regulations and attention to ethics go hand in hand. As we will discuss throughout this book, there are rules for researcher behavior, and some of them even have the force of law. However, how to apply the rules may not be obvious in every unique situation. Therefore, researchers must have a good understanding of ethics—ethical principles, theories, and frameworks—to help them determine what to do when the federal research regulations and professional ethics codes are not specific enough.

More questions? See #1, #3, and #7.

What Are the Potential Consequences of Ignoring Ethical Principles and Regulations?

When ethical standards are ignored, the potential consequences to participants and their communities, researchers, institutions, and the scientific record are myriad. Not complying with research regulations may increase the potential for participants to be harmed—physically, socially, or psychologically (see much more on potential harms in Part 2). For example, if guidelines for protecting the confidentiality of sensitive research data are not followed, there is a greater chance of a data breach, which could result in potential social, economic, or legal harms.

Serious consequences to researchers, a research study, or an institution may follow from noncompliance, regardless of whether harm to participants actually results. In cases of noncompliance, the institutional review board (IRB; the oversight body responsible for ensuring that research with human participants is conducted safely and ethically) may stop a research study. The IRB may also require that previously collected data be destroyed and not used in analysis and publication. Depending on the study, this may mean that certain data must be collected again, resulting in a loss of both time and significant use of resources. It may also mean that the research is not completed.

Depending on the severity of noncompliance, investigators who violate research rules may lose their jobs—or in the case of students, their standing in an academic program. An individual found guilty of not following federal research regulations may lose the privilege of applying for future federal research funding, and may even be fined or have to pay back grant funds. In some rare cases, researchers have served time in prison for making up their data or have been named as defendants in civil lawsuits brought by former research participants. Media outlets often cover cases involving alleged abuse of research participants.

Media reports of researchers breaking rules can result in the loss of public trust. This may in turn lead to decreased public funding to support research. Additionally, if the public loses trust in researchers, they may be unwilling to participate in research, making it difficult for researchers to recruit sufficient numbers of participants needed to answer important research questions and improve science and society.

More questions? See #7, #9, and, #96.

What Kinds of Research Are Considered Unethical, and What Are Some Examples of Serious Ethical Lapses in Social and Behavioral Sciences Research?

On a broad level, researchers may be criticized, and their research may even be considered unethical if

- the research plan/protocol is not approved by an institutional review board (IRB) prior to beginning the research;
- guidelines for obtaining informed consent are not followed appropriately;
- people are included in research without their prior consent or knowledge, when consent is required;
- researchers lie to participants (except in IRB-approved research that involves legitimate deception and appropriate debriefing processes);
- individuals are coerced into participating in research against their will;
- researchers target individuals who may find it difficult to refuse participation due to personal circumstances;
- participants are exposed to unreasonable or unnecessary risks;
- researchers do not follow their IRB-approved protocol; or
- researchers make up or manipulate research data in order to suggest promising results.

Research may still be considered unethical even if the researcher's actions do not result in clear evidence of harm or there did not appear to be any intentional wrongdoing. It is also important to realize that participants may be unintentionally harmed, even if policies and procedures are followed completely and research is conducted ethically.

The development of federal research regulations and of codes of ethics for professional societies in the social and behavioral sciences has been heavily influenced by several famous examples of serious ethical lapses that occurred before regulations existed. These are described below.

The Milgram Obedience Study. In the early 1960s, Yale University psychologist Stanley Milgram recruited people to participate in a study that was supposedly about learning. Participants were asked to administer test questions to an individual located in another room, whom they met prior to starting. If a question was answered incorrectly, the participant was told to administer a shock to the individual. The voltage of the shock increased with each incorrect answer. As the shocks increased, the individual in the other room receiving the shocks would scream and ask the participant to stop. However, the researcher, who was in the room with the participant, would simply tell them to continue and to finish asking the remaining questions. What the participants did not know was that the individual in the other room was not another participant but rather a confederate: that is, someone hired by the researcher to pretend to be in pain. What Milgram was really testing was whether and to what extent the participants would continue to obey the researcher, even when they heard pleas to stop. Some participants stopped after hearing their victim's protests; but most continued, demonstrating the potential strength of obedient tendencies. Milgram's study contributed greatly to our understanding of human psychology. However, these experiments upset some participants and have been criticized by the scientific community as psychologically harmful as well as uncomfortable, manipulative, and embarrassing. Even worse, Milgram failed to adequately debrief study participants; he did not explain the reasons for the deception and addressing their emotional distress.

The "Tearoom Trade" Study. In the mid-1960s, Laud Humphreys, a graduate student in sociology at Washington University in St. Louis, concealed his identity as a researcher and served as a lookout for male strangers having sex in public restrooms—a phenomenon referred to at the time as the "tearoom trade." By volunteering to act as a lookout, a common practice, Humphreys was able to observe men leaving the scene and getting into their cars; he would then write down their license plate numbers in order to learn their names and home addresses. He later visited some of the men at their homes, where he gathered additional demographic information about them and their families by pretending to be conducting a health department survey. Some praise Humphreys's work, published in 1975, which provided data to dispel the prevailing stereotype of homosexuals as deviants. Most of the men Humphreys followed were otherwise average members of society and, in some cases, upstanding community role models. Although there is no evidence that anyone was directly harmed or outed by the study, many sociologists have criticized Humphreys's behavior as an extreme invasion of privacy.

The Stanford Prison Study. In the early 1970s, psychologist Philip Zimbardo recruited students at Stanford University to participate in a study exploring the reasons for conflict between military guards and prisoners. Participants were assigned roles as either guards or prisoners and were placed in a simulated prison environment intended to last all day and night for two weeks. After several days, numerous participants—both guards and prisoners—expressed a desire to stop because they became so upset by the role-playing. Initially, Zimbardo would not allow the participants to leave the simulated prison environment, which was a clear violation of the principle of respect for persons. Eventually, the research was stopped after six days.

Unfortunately, ethical lapses and controversies in research are not just a historical problem. They continue to happen. Several examples of more recent controversial social and behavioral sciences studies are included in the References and Resources section for Part 1. For example, concerns have arisen about researchers' knowledge of and even participation in illegal activities (Goffman, 2014) as well as exploitation of study participants (Good, 1991).

More questions? See #21, #48, and #61.

How Do Standard Ethical Practices for Research Vary Among Academic Disciplines in the Social and Behavioral Sciences?

Although the federal research regulations were initially formulated for medical research, they also apply to social and behavioral sciences research. However, the regulations do not specifically address all methods and approaches used by social and behavioral science researchers. To provide additional guidance, professional scientific societies including the American Psychological Association, the American Sociological Association, and the American Anthropological Association have issued discipline-specific ethical codes for research. These codes can be found on the associations' websites; some are listed in the References and Resources section.

In general, there is a great deal of agreement among professional codes of research ethics across the many disciplines that fall under the broad umbrella of social and behavioral sciences, although certain fields apply different research methodologies or encounter populations that may require specific ethical consideration. For example, deception is a common practice in social psychology research. The American Psychological Association's *Ethical Principles of Psychologists and Code of Conduct* delineates conditions that must be met in order for deception of research participants to be ethically permissible, and it offers guidance on debriefing research participants who have been deceived. For research in educational settings, researchers follow the *Code of Ethics* of the American Educational Research Association, which addresses the unique issues that arise when teachers conduct research with their own students or subordinates.

Professional codes of ethics are not enforceable, but they are necessary for the ethical implementation of research. A professional code's detailed examination of specific issues pertaining to a particular discipline provides guidance regarding the acceptable and expected behavior of researchers using discipline-specific methods and approaches.

More questions? See #4, #33, and #61.

Who Is Responsible for Ensuring Research Is Conducted Ethically?

All persons involved in conducting research, whether they are the lead researcher of a study (called the principal investigator, or PI), or a research assistant working for the PI, are obligated to follow all the ethical rules for research. However, the PI has primary responsibility for what happens during the research. Students conducting research for their thesis or dissertation may have a faculty advisor, but the student has primary responsibility for the protection of research participants. No matter who funds the research, who is conducting it, and what specific form of review is required by an institutional review board (IRB), researchers (PIs, research assistants, and student investigators) must adhere to the basic principles of respect for persons, beneficence, and justice.

Federal research regulations are enforced through a system of local review by an IRB. An IRB is a committee that reviews research to ensure the safety and well-being of human research participants. IRB is the name designated for such committees in the United States. Internationally such committees may also be called research ethics boards (REBs) or committees (RECs). IRBs are located at institutions where research is conducted, such as at universities. Large research institutions may have multiple IRBs. The IRB submission and review process is discussed in detail in Part 8.

An IRB's primary responsibility is to review planned research studies before they are conducted. This review aims to ensure a favorable balance of risk and benefits; minimization of risks to participants; fair recruitment practices that do not exploit particular groups; and adequate plans to secure valid, voluntary, informed consent when necessary. No recruitment, enrollment, or data collection may begin until an IRB reviews the research study.

In the United States, if research is conducted or supported by a federal government agency (such as the National Science Foundation or the Department of Education), or if data collected will be submitted to the Food and Drug Administration (FDA), then IRB review is required by law. However, academic research institutions almost always require that all human research conducted by students, faculty, and staff members undergo some type of IRB review, regardless of funding source or type.

Because federal research regulations and professional codes do not dictate specific requirements for all situations in research, institutions that conduct research also develop and disseminate their own detailed policies. These policies must be consistent with the federal regulations; but they may include additional requirements, some of which are more stringent than the federal regulations. Researchers are expected to follow their institution-specific policies in addition to the federal regulations.

More questions? See #6, #10, and #81.

When I Begin Developing My Research, What Ethical Issues Should I First Consider?

This book provides tips for addressing specific ethical issues that may arise in social and behavioral sciences research, but how do you know which issues are relevant to your research? For all your studies, you must first and foremost demonstrate respect for participants. This may be accomplished by obtaining informed consent for participation, although consent may take a variety of forms, and in some cases, may not be required. More on this in Part 5. You must also ensure that your research has the potential to do more good than harm. Research poses a variety of risks. More on this in Part 2. You must ensure that you are fair in your selection of research participants. This is covered in Part 6. Where to begin!? Consider your topic area, target population, methods, and data sources. Here are some questions to help you get started.

What is the focus of your research, and what kinds of information do you want to collect? Will you be asking about or be in a position to observe illegal or socially stigmatized behavior? Will you learn information about people that they might not want shared with others? Even if you're not asking people about illegal or stigmatized behaviors, you might be asking them to tell you information that they consider personal and private. What people perceive as personal and private varies greatly, so avoid making assumptions about participants' needs. In any study, regardless of the topic, researchers must follow best practices to protect participants' privacy and the confidentiality of their data. More on this in Part 3.

Who is your target population? Might some or all of the individuals you want to recruit have difficulty understanding what the research is about and their rights as participants (including the right to say "no") because of either cognitive deficits, limited English proficiency, or young age? Might some have a difficult time saying "no" to participating because you are in a relationship with unequal power? More on ethical considerations and best practices for research with a variety of vulnerable populations in Part 4.

How will you find your participants? What research method (or methods) do you plan to use? Self-administered online surveys, face-to-face or telephone interviews, focus groups, or observations? Each poses unique ethical challenges. For example, focus groups limit your ability to maintain participants' privacy and the confidentiality of their data. Using deception in research may help you to collect more reliable information from participants, but you must consider ethical trade-offs. More on ethical issues to think about when designing your research in Part 6 and implementing your research in Part 10.

What will be your primary sources of data? Surveys? Observations? Data that exist in cyberspace? More on unique ethical challenges posed by different types of data sources in Parts 7 and 9.

Lastly, as you begin thinking about conducting a research study, you must find out the requirements and process for ethical review at your institution. More on the institutional review board submission process in Part 8.

More questions? See #11, #18, and #34.

PART 2

ASSESSING RESEARCH RISKS AND BENEFITS

What Is Risk, and What Are the Risks in Social and Behavioral Sciences Research?

Risk is defined as the possibility of something happening that is in some way harmful. Risk has two parts: the magnitude or degree of harm that might occur, and the probability that it will occur.

In research, risks are harms or discomforts that study participants could potentially experience from taking part in the research. As in life, where individuals experience some level of risk every day, participating in research always has risks. In most social and behavioral sciences research, the probability of harm is low, and the magnitude of potential harms is small. Therefore, most social and behavioral sciences research meets the definition of minimal risk research (see Question #13), which may affect certain requirements for institutional review board oversight and informed consent. However, despite the fact that risk is generally low, it is important for all social and behavioral sciences researchers to carefully assess risk in each study, no matter what their discipline, topic, method, or target population.

When thinking about types of risks in research, we often think first of physical harms, such as pain or bruising from having blood drawn or unpleasant side effects from taking an experimental drug. For research in the social and behavioral sciences, physical harm from study participation is usually not a concern. However, researchers in the social and behavioral sciences must think about other types of risks, including potential psychological, economic, legal, social, and dignitary harms. Potential group-level harms should also be considered.

Some harms may occur during the collection of research data. For example, psychological harms are emotional responses such as sadness, anxiety, or embarrassment that may result from sharing information with researchers.

Other types of harms may occur if a research participant's sensitive personal information is revealed to people outside of the study (see Part 3: Protecting Privacy and Confidentiality). Informational and identity breaches may result in economic, legal, or other social harms. Economic harms include negative effects on employment, such as loss of employment, or on future employability. For example, an employer may develop a negative perception of a participant because of inappropriately disclosed research findings and therefore not hire him or her. Economic harms may also include loss of business or sales, for example, if customers learn from inappropriately disclosed research findings that a business owner previously engaged in illegal behavior.

Legal harms could include arrest, imprisonment, or other legal action such as losing custody of one's children. For example, mandatory reporting laws require individuals in certain professions, such as teachers and social workers, to report any known child abuse. If research participants disclose to a mandatory reporter during research that they are neglecting their children, researchers are required to report them to the appropriate authorities.

Social harms occur when participants' relationships with others or their reputations are negatively affected because of the research. For example, if a woman is participating in a research telephone interview and her husband overhears responses to questions about her sexual history, this could damage trust between them.

Research may also include the risk of dignitary harm. This refers to the idea that people can be "wronged" without actually suffering tangible harm. For example, some people may feel violated if their academic records or social media postings are accessed without their permission, even if the information is kept safe and confidential by researchers. Some people might feel offended if a research staff member asks them a personal question, for example, about their income, sexuality, or political views.

In some cases, the publication of research findings—even if individual participant identities are appropriately de-identified—could lead individuals or communities that share characteristics with participants to be viewed negatively by others. For example, a finding that a certain group of people has higher rates of drug use may stigmatize the entire group and result in social harm, even to those individuals who did not participate in the research. These types of group-level risks are important for researchers to keep in mind when planning a research study. Engaging members of the community and asking them how to anticipate and minimize such group-level risks may help in these situations.

More questions? See #12, #23, and #63.

How Do I Identify Risks in My Research—and Minimize Them?

No matter what kind of research you are doing, you have a responsibility when designing and conducting research to (a) identify risks of participation, (b) consider the likelihood and magnitude of those risks, and (c) implement procedures to minimize those risks. When identifying risks for a particular research study, start by considering the topic under investigation and the methods of data collection and storage.

Social and behavioral sciences researchers investigate many different phenomena. Some topics of inquiry are quite benign, such as reasons people visit national parks. Such research likely has few risks. However, other kinds of research, such as interviewing individuals who are engaged in criminal activity, can be quite sensitive. In these situations, participants could feel anxious when describing past illegal activities (psychological risk). If others learned that a participant engaged in these activities, they may no longer trust the participant (social risk). Employers may be hesitant to hire the individual because of his or her previous illegal behavior (economic risk). In reality, most research asks about experiences, behavior, and opinions that fall somewhere between visiting national parks and engaging in criminal activity.

Beyond the specific topic of inquiry, you must consider risks that might arise from the methods used to identify and recruit participants and gather information. In the social and behavioral sciences, one of the main risks to consider is a potential violation of a person's privacy. You must consider the psychological, legal, economic, or social harms that could potentially result if others learned that an individual was participating in—or was just being invited to participate in—a specific research study. For example, participants could be seen entering a drug treatment facility for a study interview, which might be embarrassing or stigmatizing (social risk). Or, participants' employment (economic risk) or custody of their children (legal risk) could be jeopardized if someone sees them filling out a mailed or online survey about their drug use.

Risks from a breach in confidentiality of data are also important to consider. Participants could be harmed if unauthorized persons gained access to information collected as part of the study. For example, public embarrassment and marital discord could occur if personal data acknowledging a marital affair became public (say, for example, if data collected online were not appropriately protected). In research on employee job satisfaction, economic harm could occur and participants could lose their jobs, for example, if their supervisors learned of their dissatisfaction with the company's sick leave policies.

A variety of methods can help you identify risks and take steps to minimize them. Conduct literature reviews of research studies with similar populations or those that used similar methods. Consult with experienced researchers who have conducted similar research. Talk with individuals who share characteristics with or represent the views of prospective participants to identify what risks they think the research might pose.

Once risks are identified, you must consider the likelihood and magnitude of those risks. Unfortunately, such estimation is not an exact science. Some probabilities can be determined based on systematically collected information. However, many probabilities—especially risks of extremely rare events—are impossible to quantify. Even when relevant empirical data on risk are available, humans' estimation of future risk is subject to many biases. We tend to overestimate risk for those things we have directly experienced or heard about recently. Different researchers and institutional review board members may judge risks differently based on their own experiences.

More questions? See #17, #22, and #23.

What Is Meant by "Minimal Risk"?

According to the federal research regulations, minimal risk "means that the probability and magnitude of harm or discomfort anticipated in the research are not greater in and of themselves than those ordinarily encountered in daily life or during the performance of routine physical or psychological examinations or tests" (45 C.F.R. § 46.102(j)). Research studies are evaluated according to whether they pose more risk than what people face when going about their normal activities. Most social and behavioral sciences research meets the definition of minimal risk. However, determining the ordinary risks of daily living is tricky. Such risks can vary depending on where people live, their health status, their jobs, and the kinds of activities in which they regularly engage.

Every research study can be considered to pose either "no more than minimal risk" or "greater than minimal risk." As described in more detail in Part 8: Negotiating the IRB Review Process, the type of institutional review board (IRB) review (exempt, expedited, or full board) that a research study must undergo is determined by whether the research study is deemed by the IRB to pose no more than minimal risk or greater than minimal risk. A comprehensive IRB application should clearly outline risks and provide information to help the IRB make the appropriate determination.

Researchers and IRBs may not always be consistent in their interpretation and application of the concept of minimal risk, due to the broad regulatory definition. For example, whose daily life should be considered—a person who represents the majority of people in a community, or a person who represents people who will likely participate in the research? Either standard may be applied by an IRB.

More questions? See #16, #77, and #79.

What Are the Potential Benefits of Research?

A research study should be conducted only if it offers some benefit to science and society: that is, it answers a new question or adds new information to what is already known. Research may also benefit those who participate. Different kinds of benefits may be offered to participants, and these should be described in the research protocol and during the consent process. In order to be ethical, research must always have potential for social or scientific benefit, but it does not have to directly benefit participants.

Some research studies provide tangible benefits, such as resources or services (related to the study's primary objective) that participants normally would not be able to access (or easily access) outside of study participation. For example, a study on weight loss may provide participants with services such as a health screening or resources such as books, step counters, scales, exercise equipment, or pre-made meals. In describing benefits to participants during recruitment and the informed consent process, financial payment for research participation should not be considered as a tangible benefit.

Participants may also receive intangible benefits from participating in a research study. Participants may learn more about a specific health issue, enjoy interacting with others, or appreciate the opportunity to share their experiences and views. For example, individuals who participate in qualitative interviews about a traumatic experience (such as domestic violence or a natural disaster) may have a positive emotional response from talking about their experience. In addition, some participants may feel good about participating in research because it may help others in the future. Similarly, participants may also benefit psychologically from participating in research, knowing that they are contributing to science or helping researchers find solutions to social problems that affect their community.

Even when there is potential to benefit from a research study, not all participants may experience benefit. As a result, some participants may regret participating in the research. Researchers must take care when describing the benefits to participants not to exaggerate their value. A good rule to follow is to state clearly that participants *may* receive some benefits, and emphasize only those benefits that all participants have an opportunity to receive.

In research that aims to evaluate the effects of an educational or behavioral intervention, researchers should not promise benefits in the form of specific outcomes. Consider, for example, the study of an educational intervention that aims to improve reading scores among elementary school children. If the research demonstrates that the intervention is efficacious, some participants who received the experimental intervention will in fact have received a benefit from research participation, that is, improved reading scores. However, researchers should not promise that children's reading scores will improve if they participate in the study because the real purpose of intervention research is to gather data to determine the efficacy or effectiveness of an intervention so that individuals *in the future* can benefit, not individuals in the study. And even the best interventions do not work for everyone who tries them. Further, intervention research often includes a control group, which means that only some participants receive the experimental intervention, and others receive a placebo or no intervention—and therefore the likelihood of any benefit is low for those in the control group.

Research can offer benefits not only to those who participate, but also to the community in which the research is conducted. Such benefits can be tangible, such as paid employment opportunities, or intangible, such as development of research capacity. All kinds of research, regardless of the findings, ideally benefits science and society. For example, surveys, interviews, and ethnographic studies can identify root causes or correlational factors for social problems. Or, if an intervention is shown to be efficacious, it can be offered widely to benefit other individuals in the community and elsewhere. If the intervention is shown not to be efficacious, science still benefits because researchers can rule out what does not work; society benefits because citizens will not be offered (and their tax dollars will not pay for) programs that do not work.

More questions? See #15, #16, and #62.

How Do I Design My Research So That the Risk–Benefit Balance Is Favorable?

The federal research regulations require that institutional review boards (IRBs) determine that the "[r]isks to subjects are reasonable in relation to anticipated benefits, if any, to subjects, and the importance of the knowledge that may reasonably be expected to result" (45 C.F.R. § 46.111(2)) from the research. This means that participants should not be subjected to risks when participating in research without the prospect of some benefit. Research does not have to provide direct benefits to those who participate, but there must be some potential benefit to science and society.

While there is no magic formula for determining a reasonable balance between research risks and potential benefits, you must honestly consider the following:

- the anticipated risks of study participation;
- the likelihood and magnitude of those risks, and steps you will take to minimize those risks;
- the potential expected benefits of the research to participants; and
- the potential knowledge that will be gained by your study.

When designing your research study, you will want to make sure you have clearly thought through all these issues and that, from your perspective, the potential benefits outweigh the risks. You will also want to ensure that this information is clearly described in your protocol, so the IRB has sufficient knowledge to make their determination. It is important to keep in mind that IRBs may view the risks and benefits of a particular study differently from the researcher who designed the study. Perceptions of risks and benefits may also vary among the different members of an IRB.

More questions? See #11, #12, and #14.

How Do I Make Sure That Participants in My Research Do Not Overestimate the Benefits or Underestimate the Risks?

The term "therapeutic misconception" is used to describe when research participants incorrectly assume that they will directly benefit from taking part in a research study. However, the primary purpose of research is to gather generalizable knowledge to help people in the future; direct benefits cannot be assumed. The therapeutic misconception can occur if a participant does not fully understand the purpose of the research, or does not understand the differences between research and services. Individuals participating in research may incorrectly believe that the intervention or program being evaluated in a research study already has an evidence base to support its use. They may not realize that they are being asked to participate in research in order to gather needed evidence on whether the intervention works—or does not work.

Although the term was conceived of within the context of clinical research, therapeutic misconception can occur in social and behavioral sciences research. Researchers should be particularly aware of the potential for such misunderstanding when conducting research on behavioral or educational interventions. People tend to assume that any services offered are already proven to help. When recruiting for an intervention study, it is especially important to emphasize that you do not yet know if the intervention being offered will achieve the desired results.

Participants may also misunderstand the purpose of the research in nonexperimental studies that use surveys or interviews. For example, individuals might confuse a request to take a survey about their smoking habits with an offer to participate in a program designed to help them quit. Being asked to take part in an in-depth qualitative interview after a natural disaster could be mistaken for an offer of counseling or other mental health services. The potential for such conflation is particularly strong if the study is being conducted by a service provider or in collaboration with an agency that provides direct services.

The best way to limit potential misconceptions about research is to provide participants with clear information about the purpose and benefits of the research during the recruitment and informed consent process. For example, to explain the study purpose, you can include straightforward statements such as, "The purpose of the study is to find out if this program can help students improve their reading scores. We do not know if this program is better or worse than the current reading program offered. We are doing the research to answer this question." Regarding benefits, you can include statements such as, "You will not receive any direct benefit from taking part in this research. However, if we find out that the program works, it can be offered to students in the future."

More questions? See #11, #14, and #40.

I Will Conduct Research on a Sensitive Topic. What Should I Do to Prevent Psychological Harms?

Research in the social and behavioral sciences may explore sensitive topics. A few examples include domestic violence, sexual assault, sexual practices, or the death of a loved one. Such research poses psychological risks such as sadness, anxiety, or embarrassment. You can take several steps to reduce the possibility that participants experience psychological harm from participating in research on sensitive topics.

You should consider the method of data collection, as different methods carry different kinds of risks. The thorough exploration of past experiences through in-depth interviews may increase the risk of psychological harm compared with surveys, which are usually more superficial. However, in-depth interviews involve a relational aspect that might provide greater opportunities for participants to make meaning of their experiences and thereby increase participants' perceived benefits and contribution to science as compared with surveys. Conducting face-to-face, in-depth interviews also includes the possibility of other risks, such as a breach of privacy because the participants' identities are known by the researcher, and they may be seen by others.

Methods to reduce the possibility of psychological harm include

- limiting the number of sensitive questions included in a survey or interview guide to the most essential;
- during the informed consent process, describing the types of questions that will be asked so potential participants can decline if they feel that the questions are too intrusive or that they might become upset from answering the questions; and
- letting participants know ahead of time that they can choose not to answer any question that makes them feel uncomfortable.

If a participant becomes upset, it is a good practice to stop the survey or interview—if it is a face-to-face or telephone interaction—and allow the participant time to regain composure. If in person, interviewers should offer the participant tissues and a glass of water. Once the participant is ready, the interview or survey can resume. However, participants should be allowed to stop the interview or survey completely if they do not want to continue. In these situations, the interviewer should obtain the participant's permission to allow any data provided thus far to be included in the research—even if a consent form has been signed. If participants decline, their data should not be included in the dataset. Even when the survey or interview was not completed, interviewers should provide the participant with the reimbursement or incentive for completing the interview or survey.

Identifying and minimizing psychological harm can be trickier in research that is not conducted in person, particularly for online surveys, because the researcher will not know if the participant becomes upset. For research conducted in any setting, when applicable, researchers should arrange for referral to counselors and list community programs for any participants who want such services—even for those who do not become upset during the research. These services can be described to participants at the end of the survey/interview or earlier, if appropriate.

More questions? See #11, #12, and #97.

PART 3

PROTECTING PRIVACY AND CONFIDENTIALITY

What Is Meant by "Privacy" and "Confidentiality," and Is There a Difference?

Privacy and confidentiality are two critical concepts that all researchers must address when designing and implementing research. Often assumed to have the same meaning, privacy and confidentiality are, in fact, two discrete but related concepts. An easy way to distinguish the two is to think of privacy as protecting individuals and confidentiality as protecting information—or data—that people share with researchers.

Privacy can be defined as having control over oneself—that is, people can choose when to share information about themselves and with whom. During recruitment, you can protect the privacy of prospective participants by implementing procedures that do not disclose information to others that would identify prospective participants as being part of a specific group, engaging in a specific behavior, or having a specific health condition. During data collection, you can reduce the likelihood of a violation of privacy by implementing procedures that allow participants to share their information with researchers where others cannot hear or see them.

When participants privately share their information with researchers, they expect that their information will remain confidential—that is, they expect that only the research team and other authorized individuals will have access to their data. In a practical sense, confidentiality refers to the specific steps researchers implement to keep information about participants unknown to others, to the extent possible. Federal research regulations require researchers to establish procedures to protect the confidentiality of information that is individually identifiable (meaning, the participant can be identified directly by the researcher or through identifiers that are linked with the data). However, researchers often implement the same confidentiality procedures for all types of data, as they are good standard research practices.

More questions? See #21, #22, and #23.

What Makes Data De-Identified?

Datasets that have been stripped of all personal identifiers are considered to be de-identified. The federal research regulations do not list specific personal identifiers. Instead, they loosely define identifiable to mean that "the identity of the subject is or may readily be ascertained by the investigator or associated with the information" (45 C.F.R. § 46.102(e) (5)). Although a universal list of personal identifiers does not exist, the 18 identifiers listed in the Health Insurance Portability and Accountability Act (HIPAA) Privacy Rule (such as participant name and date of birth) are reasonable identifiers that researchers should consider removing from their datasets when de-identifying them (USHHS, 2015a, 2015b).

The premise of de-identifying datasets is that by removing all personal identifiers, the participants' identities likely cannot be determined by those who see the data. Even after datasets are de-identified, however, a slight risk remains that participants can be re-identified, if someone had the interest in and means to do so. Therefore, researchers and ethicists debate the extent to which data can truly be de-identified.

Typically researchers must de-identify their datasets when they plan to share them with researchers outside the original study team (such as for secondary data analysis), when the data are to be made publicly available, or when they prepare data for long-term storage. Adequately de-identifying datasets may take considerable effort, depending on the type of information collected. Numerous procedures exist for removing or masking identifiers in *quantitative* datasets. For example, a specific process is required for removing all HIPAA identifiers from quantitative datasets in research that must follow the HIPAA Privacy Rule (USHHS, 2015a, 2015b).

Processes for de-identifying *qualitative* data are not as straightforward. Overall, it is very difficult to de-identify qualitative data. Researchers typically modify easily-identifiable data in interview transcripts. For example, proper names said by the participant, such as "my friend Bob," are removed and replaced with a general description ("my friend") or a pseudonym. However, that step alone likely does not make qualitative data de-identified. Larger segments, including very specific or unusual experiences, may need to be redacted from transcripts to preserve participants' identities. Social and behavioral scientists must therefore be mindful of the quality of their data—both quantitative and qualitative—if a large amount of stripping must be done to de-identify them, and whether the necessary context will still remain to allow for valid interpretations to be made by others.

When de-identifying data for sharing or storage, the master list linking personal identifiers to the study data does not necessarily have to be destroyed. Institutional review boards often allow the original researcher to maintain the master list that links the participants' names to their identification numbers, but that list must be stored securely and not shared.

More questions? See #18, #20, and #24.

What Makes Data Anonymous?

Data are anonymous when they are not linked to any participant identifiers. In other words, the identity of a participant cannot be determined through his or her data. If the data are truly anonymous, even the study team cannot determine participants' identities. Researchers often choose to collect data anonymously for studies on stigmatized or illegal behaviors. Then, if unauthorized persons gain access to the data—or if the data were purposefully shared with other researchers for secondary analyses—participants' identities could not be detected because identifying information was never collected or known by the researchers at all. Importantly, data do not need to be anonymous to be considered ethical; employing secure procedures for limiting a confidentiality breach of identifiable data is ethically sufficient. Only in certain situations where extra protections are needed is it preferable to collect data anonymously. However, some researchers—regardless of whether the research topic is sensitive or not—choose to collect data anonymously for a study because they do not need participants' identifiers to answer their research questions.

If you want to collect data anonymously, you must consider several factors. First, your study design matters. Collecting anonymous data is likely an unrealistic option for research that requires data to be linked from multiple interactions with the same participant, such as in longitudinal research. In these situations, researchers should keep a master list linking participant names to their participant identification numbers so they can ensure that data are collected from the same participant at each time point. Participants can therefore be identified by anyone who has access to this list. Researchers who want their data to be anonymous should consider employing a study design that has only a single interaction with participants, such as a one-time interview or survey.

Second, consider how you are going to collect data. Collecting anonymous data is not possible when you (or another member of the research team) meet in person with a participant to conduct an interview or survey, for example. By conducting a face-to-face interview, you know what the person looks like and therefore can identify him or her, even if you do not know the participant's name or have any other identifiers. Depending on the topic of the study, being identified as a participant (even without any disclosure of information discussed) could be potentially stigmatizing. For similar reasons, if a researcher wants to collect data anonymously, participants can neither be video recorded nor have their pictures taken because they can be visually identified. Data from audio-recorded interviews are also not considered anonymous because participants' voices are unique, like fingerprints, and therefore considered identifiable.

Third, consider the kinds of data to be collected. For data to be anonymous, you cannot collect *any* information that can identify a participant. This information includes, for example, participant names, email addresses, and date of birth. Eighteen specific identifiers are listed in the Health Insurance Portability and Accountability Act (HIPAA) Privacy Rule (USHHS, 2015b). The Family Educational Rights and Privacy Act Regulations (FERPA) also provide a list of direct and indirect identifiers (USDE, 2017). Some identifiers may be unique to a particular study participant, such as a description of a tattoo, and when known, could identify the participant. A combination of identifiers when viewed together, such as ethnicity, sexual orientation, and age, could also reveal the identity of a study participant in some situations, especially when research is conducted in small towns or communities.

Data that were originally collected with personal identifiers can become anonymous data, in theory, if all personal identifiers are removed from the data *and any documents linking identities and data are destroyed.*

Ultimately, it may be difficult to collect data that are truly anonymous. Often researchers want to know identifying information to provide context to the data or to maintain long-term contact with participants. If you need to collect participant identifiers but are concerned about the negative implications of others potentially discovering the identities of participants in your research study, use strict procedures to protect the confidentiality of study data and consider obtaining verbal consent, so that participants' names are not linked to the study though their signature on a consent form.

More questions? See #19, #23, and #25.

When Is Information (or Behavior) Considered Private Rather Than Public, and How Can Private Information Be Used in Research?

When information is provided in a private place, such as when a patient tells his doctor that he is feeling depressed during a medical checkup, the patient has a reasonable expectation that the information will remain private and will not be used for other purposes, such as for research. The federal research regulations state that "[p]rivate information includes information about behavior that occurs in a context in which an individual can reasonably expect that no observation or recording is taking place, and information that has been provided for specific purposes by an individual and that the individual can reasonably expect will not be made public (e.g., a medical record)" (45 C.F.R. § 46.102(e)(4)). When information is provided in a public space—especially nonsensitive information, such as when a person comments on an online news story—people's expectations of privacy are typically much lower.

Other situations, however, are not as straightforward, particularly when people share information they perceive to be private in public places. For instance, is it ethical for researchers to listen to and use for research purposes a conversation between two friends at a coffee shop, without their consent? Even though the individuals are communicating in a public space, they may believe that their conversation is private and have a perception that this information will remain private—that is, no one else is listening and documenting what they are saying. As a researcher, a good question to ask yourself is: Would these individuals feel that their privacy has been violated if they learned a researcher was using what they said for research purposes?

In examining these situations through the lens of the federal research regulations, conversations between patients and their doctors are considered private, and researchers are not allowed to use that information as data for their study, unless they obtain the patient's consent or do not collect any identifiable information about the patient. Similarly, a conversation between two people at a coffee shop would be considered private information, because the people would reasonably expect that their conversation would not be recorded, made public, or included in a research study without their knowledge. However, researchers could still observe and analyze this information, as long as they do not link any identifiable information with the conversation data. Comments made online in a public forum and public speeches would be considered public information and generally can be used for research purposes without obtaining informed consent.

More questions? See #60, #70, and #72.

What Can I Do to Protect Participants' Privacy During Data Collection and Reporting?

During data collection, you must limit the possibility that others will see participants taking part in research activities or will hear the information that they are sharing in an interview. As a general rule, all research interactions should be conducted in a private location where the conversation cannot be seen or heard by others. However, it is often desirable to hold study interviews in a neutral location, such as a public library. This is acceptable as long as privacy is maintained. While infrequent, participants may want someone else such as a spouse or other family member present during their interview. From a privacy perspective, this is allowed if it is requested by the participant. However, you will need to consider other factors: How sensitive are the questions being asked? Will the other person share information discussed in the interview with others? Is it possible that the participant may be less truthful in front of this other person? If the answer to any of these questions is "yes," then it may be best not to include this person in your research.

When reporting your research findings, data must be presented in a way that prevents individual participants from being identified. This is especially important in qualitative research where participant quotes are typically provided to illustrate an aspect of the data. While it is ethically acceptable to include participants' demographics with the quotes, such as the participant's gender and age, you must evaluate whether the context provided in the quote combined with demographic data could potentially identify the participant. Additionally, it may be difficult to conceal participants' identities when the research is conducted in small towns or communities. In some situations, it may also be difficult to conceal the geographic location of a study population when the authors' affiliations are included with the manuscript or are easily searchable online. You should consider these factors when deciding what information about participants—and which parts of quotes—to include when describing the findings from qualitative research.

More questions? See #56, #59, and #72.

What Can I Do to Protect the Confidentiality of Information Collected?

Researchers must implement procedures to limit the likelihood that people outside the study team can gain access to information shared by participants during research. Confidentiality of participant data can never be fully protected or guaranteed, as unanticipated breaches can occur due to human error. A study computer may be stolen, data might be stored on servers that are not secure or password protected, field notes may be lost, or transcripts might be left on the data analyst's desk at the end of the day. These errors allow unauthorized people to gain access to and read participant information.

Fortunately, there are several basic steps that can be taken to substantially limit the likelihood of a breach in confidentiality:

- Use participant identification numbers instead of participant names on all hard copy and electronic study documents, including surveys, field notes, photographs, and audio and video recordings.
- Collect only those personal identifiers that are absolutely necessary. If risk of a breach of data would pose significant harm to participants, consider collecting no personal identifiers.
- Breaches of confidentiality may happen during transport. After collecting data in the field, return to the study office immediately with any completed questionnaires, field notes, and recording devices to appropriately log and store them. If possible, upload the audio recordings to a secure location in the cloud prior to leaving the data collection site. Erase interviews from recording devices as soon as audio files are stored on a secure server.
- Password protect all electronic document files, and store them on secure servers or password-protected computers.
- Store all hard copy research records—such as handwritten interview notes and printed transcripts—in locked cabinets.

- Avoid storing any research records on portable USB flash drives. If such storage is temporarily necessary, the records should be copied to a secure server as soon as possible and deleted from the less secure temporary storage devices.
- Limit access to study files to essential study staff.
- Keep signed consent forms and other documents that include participant names, such as master participant lists and contact information sheets, separate from documents containing participant data. Hard copies of these files should be stored in separate, locked cabinets. Electronic files should be kept in separate electronic folders and have different passwords; for example, the same password should not be used for interview transcripts and the master participant list.
- If re-identification will not be necessary, destroy all documents that would allow for the re-identification of participants, such as the master list of participant identifiers, as soon as possible after research is complete.

More questions? See #25, #88, and #99.

When Must I Share Study Data—and Participant Names—With Individuals Outside of the Research Team?

While uncommon in the social and behavioral sciences, there are circumstances in which people outside of the study team may need to look at your research data. For example, an institutional review board (IRB) may need to review study data to investigate participant complaints of mistreatment or accusations of data falsification/fabrication. Funding agencies are also typically allowed to view study data if deemed necessary. To inform prospective participants that people outside of the study team may have access to their data, researchers often disclose, during the informed consent process, all the possible groups that may have access to research data. This way, participants are fully informed of who may see their information when they make their decision about research participation.

You may be required to share research data—and participant names—with individuals outside of the research team when it is necessary to ensure the safety of the participant or others. State laws vary, but most require certain individuals, referred to as "mandatory reporters," such as medical doctors, nurses, teachers, guidance counselors, and social workers, to share any disclosure of child or elder abuse or neglect with authorities. In these situations, a breach in confidentiality and privacy may be necessary to protect participant safety or the safety of others.

If it is possible that participants may disclose information about their own safety or the safety of others during the course of your research, you should investigate your state laws, engage your local IRB, and contact legal counsel at your institution. You'll need to determine if you are considered a mandatory reporter and to ensure that your research follows all applicable laws and professional ethical requirements. When conducting research on a topic that could lead to the disclosure of reportable information, prospective participants must be informed during the consent process that any information they share about potential harm to themselves or others will be reported to the authorities, and that this could result in legal action against them.

More questions? See #25, #93, and #94.

What Is a Certificate of Confidentiality?

A Certificate of Confidentiality (CoC) protects researchers from forced disclosure of participant data—including participants' identities—to local, state, and federal authorities. Researchers who have a CoC can refuse to provide information about participants when solicited by the authorities. Without a CoC in place, researchers may be legally required to disclose participants' data and identities, for example, if their data are subpoenaed for a civil or criminal case.

Regardless of who is conducting or funding the research, CoCs are issued by the National Institutes of Health (NIH, 2016) and other Department of Health and Human Services (HHS) agencies to the researcher's institution. NIH automatically issues CoCs for NIH-funded research that collects or uses identifiable, sensitive information. NIH describes "identifiable, sensitive information" to mean "information about an individual that is gathered or used during the course of biomedical, behavioral, clinical, or other research, where the following may occur: an individual is identified; or for which there is at least a very small risk, that some combination of the information, a request for the information, and other available data sources could be used to deduce the identity of an individual" (301(d) Public Health Service Act (42 U.S.C 241)). Researchers with other sources of funding may request a CoC from the NIH when they collect identifiable, sensitive information as part of health-related research.

Importantly, having a CoC in place does not mean that researchers may never share information about participants with authorities. A researcher may need to contact authorities when a participant discloses plans to harm someone, for example. A CoC prevents only involuntary and forced disclosure of research information by researchers.

More questions? See #12, #23, and #98.

What Privacy Laws Must I Follow?

If you plan to conduct research in U.S. public schools, you should become familiar with the Federal Education Rights and Privacy Act (FERPA). This federal law "affords parents the right to have access to their children's education records, the right to seek to have the records amended, and the right to have some control over the disclosure of personally identifiable information from the education records" (USDE, 2017). It outlines rules regarding informed consent that must be followed when accessing student education records for research purposes. With some exceptions, parental consent is required for researchers to access records and collect identifiable information of students who are under the age of 18 (or the age of majority in the specific state). Parental consent may not be required for collecting nonidentifiable data from student records.

If you plan to conduct research in medical settings or with patients, you should become familiar with the Health Insurance Portability and Accountability Act (HIPAA; USDHHS, 2015a, 2015b). The purpose of the HIPAA Privacy Rule is to protect information in individuals' medical records (electronic or other) as well as other personal health information provided by individuals when engaged in or paying for health care. Often information that was originally collected for health care purposes can be used to answer social and behavioral research questions. For example, if you want to analyze existing medical records data to examine the association between heart disease and mental health, or to identify patients with heart disease to participate in interviews on nutrition, you will need to follow the HIPAA Privacy Rule. If you plan to conduct research with patients or by using medical records, check with your institution to determine how to comply with the HIPAA Privacy Rule.

More questions? See #33, #52, and #53.

PART 4

PROTECTING VULNERABLE POPULATIONS

What Kinds of Participants Are Considered Vulnerable in Research, and What Are Some Ways to Protect Vulnerable Participants?

Some people may be particularly vulnerable to exploitation and harm in the context of research. Most researchers, scholars, and institutional review board (IRB) members agree that special efforts should be made to protect vulnerable individuals. While the federal research regulations address some specific populations, there is no precise formula for determining who is vulnerable, and differences of opinion exist regarding appropriate protections.

The *Belmont Report* (1979) affirms a requirement to protect "persons with diminished autonomy," referring to individuals who do not have the capacity for self-determination due to either young age, illness or disability that affects comprehension, or circumstances that may restrict their ability to voluntarily refuse to participate in research. Vulnerabilities may affect a person's ability to adequately judge the potential risks involved in participation and/or to refuse participation. However, considered broadly, vulnerability in research is about more than just capacity for self-determination. Research activities that pose minimal risk to healthy adults may be riskier for children, individuals with certain physical or mental illnesses, or individuals engaged in illegal behavior. For example, it may cause more social harm if private information about a child's sexual identity or behavior becomes known outside of research as compared with that of an adult. The topic of the research also matters. Individuals who use illegal drugs and participate in surveys about drug use are obviously at greater risk of harm from a breach of confidentiality than vegetarians who participate in surveys about fruit and vegetable intake.

The federal research regulations identify pregnant women, human fetuses, and neonates; prisoners; and children as particularly vulnerable.

Extra protections for these populations are delineated in 45 C.F.R. § 46, Subpart B (Pregnant Women, Human Fetuses and Neonates), Subpart C (Prisoners), and Subpart D (Children). Beyond these subparts, the federal regulations also direct IRBs, during the review of a research protocol, to include individuals who are knowledgeable about and have experience in working with the proposed study population; consider the special problems of research that may be involved; and include additional safeguards to protect participants who are "vulnerable to coercion or undue influence, such as children, prisoners, individuals with impaired decision-making capacity, or economically or educationally disadvantaged persons" (45 C.F.R. § 46.107(a)). Based on other research guidelines and ethics scholarship, others who may be considered vulnerable in research might include individuals

- who are patients with limited options for treatment or cure, such as patients with terminal cancer;
- who have experienced traumatic events, such as rape survivors and refugees;
- who engage in socially stigmatized or illegal behavior or are members of historically and/or politically marginalized groups, such as drug users or members of LGBTQ communities; and
- whom the researcher has disproportionate power over, such as students or employees.

This list is certainly not exhaustive; and, as we learn more about human life and behavior, new vulnerabilities that affect research participation may emerge.

Some scholars reject a categorical approach to vulnerability based on demographics (DuBois et al., 2012; Kipnis, 2001). That is, group membership should not automatically deem one to be vulnerable. Vulnerability is not something that resides within the person. Rather, vulnerability arises within particular situations. In reality, because of the inherent power differential between researchers and participants, any participant may be vulnerable to exploitation or to physical, psychological, social, or dignitary harm. The particular risks, benefits, and requirements of a given study also affect the potential vulnerability of participants and the requirement for additional protections. However, a categorical approach to vulnerability is still useful in that involvement of individuals generally considered vulnerable can alert novice researchers to the need for special considerations.

If your research involves individuals who may be considered vulnerable, you should be aware of ethically optimal protections that go beyond what is usually required for adult volunteers who are not considered vulnerable, including those protections that may be legally required. Questions #28–#33 discuss protections for specific groups of research participants, but generally, such protections may include:

- Exclusion from certain types of research. For example, prisoners are generally prohibited from participating in research when the research findings will not specifically benefit prisoner populations in the future.
- Involvement of a surrogate decision maker. Research with children generally requires parental permission. Research with adults who lack decision-making capacity may require the consent of a legally authorized representative.
- Involvement of a participant advocate. In certain circumstances, research with adolescents may be conducted without parental permission, if parental permission might be impractical or cause harm to participants, such as with homeless or LGBTQ youth. An IRB may require the presence of a participate advocate not otherwise associated with the research to help ensure adequate understanding and consideration of the risks and benefits.
- Observation or monitoring of the consent process by a third party. This may be appropriate in studies where prospective participants may have limited literacy.
- Formal assessment of comprehension of research purpose, risks, benefits, and requirements prior to enrollment. This is most appropriate in studies where inclusion criteria suggest that all or most prospective participants will have diminished decision-making capacity and the research poses greater than minimal risk.
- More frequent continuing review by an IRB, for example, every six months as opposed to every year. This may allow the IRB to determine that certain vulnerable groups are not being disproportionately enrolled or to ascertain the frequency of anticipated harms.
- Additional tests or other types of monitoring to minimize risk, such as formal screening for emotional upset.
- Research procedures that enhance participant voluntariness. For example, if teachers would like to conduct survey research with their students, surveys can be distributed and collected by a third party so that the teachers cannot determine who did and did not participate.

All research requires the balance of two important goals: protecting participants from exploitation and harm, and providing equal access to the direct and indirect benefits of research. Vulnerable populations should not be excluded from research to such an extreme that they are not able to share in its potential benefits. Researchers should not shy away from conducting research with vulnerable groups simply due to the need to be more thoughtful about ethical issues and special protections.

More questions? See #28–#33.

What Ethical Issues Should I Consider When Conducting Research With Prisoners?

Incarceration may affect a prisoner's ability to make a voluntary decision regarding research participation. Power dynamics in the prison setting may completely rule out any possibility of free choice. However, research with prisoners is needed to further society's understanding of criminal behavior and to improve the health and well-being of prisoners.

Historically, U.S. prisoners have been exploited in research. Their captivity makes conducting research—and controlling experimental conditions—extremely easy for researchers. In the 1960s and early 1970s, a large percentage of new drugs were tested on prisoners. This is no longer allowable under federal research regulations.

Many prisoners may have other characteristics that might make them additionally vulnerable in research. The U.S. prisoner population is disproportionately economically and educationally disadvantaged, and suffering from untreated medical problems, particularly psychiatric illness and addiction. Although such "co-vulnerabilities" do not necessarily render prisoners incapable of making autonomous decisions about research participation, they may require you to implement additional protections, such as easy-to-read consent forms or participant advocates. More significantly, the background conditions of prison may also increase prisoners' vulnerability in research, particularly their willingness to say "yes" to any kind of research. Such conditions include limited opportunities to earn money, excessive boredom, and limited access to health services. Additionally, inmates may want to feel like a contributing member of society or perhaps just have something to fill their time. This may lead them to agree to participate in a research study without fully considering the risks and burdens.

45 C.F.R. § 46, Subpart C (Additional Protections Pertaining to Biomedical and Behavioral Research Involving Prisoners as Subjects) spells out ethical parameters for research with prisoners. According to these regulations, a "prisoner" is defined as "any individual involuntarily confined or detained in a penal institution" (45 C.F.R. § 46.303(c)) and thus

excludes parolees as well as individuals under house arrest. Allowable research includes:

- Research on the causes and effects of criminal behavior and incarceration or studies of prisons as institutions (or of prisoners as "incarcerated persons") that pose no more than minimal risk or inconvenience to participants.
- Research on issues that affect prisoners "as a class," for example, diseases such as hepatitis or disorders such as drug addiction that disproportionately affect prisoners. However, such research may be conducted only after consultation with experts and the publication of a notice by the Secretary of the Department of Health and Human Services (HHS) of the intent to conduct such research.
- Research that is greater than minimal risk but that has the potential to provide direct benefit to prisoner participants. If such research involves participants in a control group that may not benefit from participation, then expert consultation and the HHS Secretary's public notice are also required.

Subpart C also outlines specific additional safeguards for research involving prisoners:

- Any advantages that prisoners might receive by participating in research, such as better food or the opportunity to earn money, cannot be so high as to impair their ability to weigh the risks and benefits of participation.
- Prisoners cannot be subjected to any greater research risks than would be allowable for nonprisoner research participants.
- Procedures for the selection of participants within the prison must be fair. Certain prisoners cannot be favorably selected or excluded by prison authorities (or other prisoners).
- Participation in research can have no influence on parole decisions.
- Provisions must be made for following up with participants after a study has ended. Individual sentence length must be taken into consideration, and participants must be informed of any short- or long-term follow-up plans.

Privacy and confidentiality are extremely difficult to maintain in the prison setting. Everyone knows when prisoners come and go; this makes it difficult to keep even the mere fact of participation private. If everyone in the prison knows that a particular type of study is going on or that a certain condition, such as HIV, is required for participation, a prisoner going to a certain place at a certain time could result in disclosure of personal health information and the risk of physical or emotional harm, which is already exacerbated in this population.

Researchers may also face unique challenges while working in prisons. For example, in the course of data collection or even casual conversation, a prisoner might disclose to you that they are being intimidated by another inmate or a correctional officer. If you are planning to conduct research in a prison, you should anticipate these kinds of issues and develop plans for addressing them.

Depending on the topic you are studying, participants may become incarcerated during the course of the research. For example, in a longitudinal survey study of intravenous drug users or sex workers that lasts several years, it is likely that some participants may become incarcerated. If it is likely that a significant number of participants may become incarcerated, you may want to continue their participation in the research while they are in jail or prison. If so, the extra protections for prisoners in the federal research regulations now become relevant.

More questions? See #22, #41, and #49.

What Ethical Issues Should I Consider When Conducting Research With Pregnant Women?

Women who are pregnant are considered vulnerable in research because their physiological state is different from when they are not pregnant. They therefore are assumed to have special needs. Additionally, fetuses may be subject to different risks and benefits than are pregnant women. While many oppose the universal labelling of all pregnant women as vulnerable, the federal research regulations specifically name pregnant women, human fetuses, and neonates as a vulnerable group and outline specific considerations and protections in Subpart B of 45 C.F.R. § 46 (Additional Protections for Pregnant Women, Human Fetuses and Neonates Involved in Research).

Subpart B was intended to protect pregnant women, fetuses, and neonates in medical research. Arguably, there is no good reason to believe that pregnant women would be more vulnerable than nonpregnant women in the context of most social and behavioral sciences research. Research on the experience of pregnancy and behavioral interventions to improve the health and well-being of pregnant women can provide benefits to participants and future pregnant women and their families. However, some institutional review boards take a conservative stance in their interpretation of Subpart B. This is in large part due to concerns about the effect of emotional stress on a developing baby—despite the fact that there are limited data on the potential for research activities, such as taking a survey or participating in a focus group, to increase stress in any meaningful or lasting way. Total exclusion of pregnant women from research based on perceived vulnerabilities may be unjust, especially if exclusion results in limited knowledge or applicability of research findings.

If you are conducting research with women who are or may be pregnant, is important to consider that pregnancy may be a private or sensitive matter for some women. If pregnancy is a requirement or exclusion criteria for your research, you need to ask if (and if necessary, verify that) the prospective participant is indeed pregnant in a respectful, private manner.

For example, screening questions might be answered on paper rather than in a face-to-face setting. Questions related to pregnancy (including the simple question: Are you pregnant?) should not be asked in public places where others can overhear. Also, pregnancy should never be assumed based on a woman's appearance.

More questions? See #17, #22, and #50.

What Ethical Issues Should I Consider When Conducting Research With Children?

Historically, the inability of children (in most U.S. states, those who are younger than 18 years of age) to protect themselves has made them vulnerable to exploitation by researchers. Children are not "tiny adults." Research that poses no greater than minimal risk to adults may pose greater risks to children. And, in many cases, children require specific interventions or solutions to their health and social problems. Research with children is therefore necessary to provide information regarding appropriate solutions for problems affecting children.

45 C.F.R. § 46, Subpart D (Additional Protections for Children Involved as Subjects in Research), addresses the upper limits of risks to which children can be exposed in research. In general, in order to be approvable under the current federal research regulations, research with children should pose no greater than minimal risk, unless it offers direct benefit. However, if a planned research study poses a minor increase over minimal risk but no prospect of direct benefit, the research may be allowable if it is likely to yield generalizable knowledge about a condition or illness that will benefit future individuals. For example, qualitative interviews that ask children diagnosed with terminal illness to discuss their experiences of hospital versus home care may be viewed as posing a risk of potential distress—a minor increase over minimal risk, but this research may be the only way to gain valuable information to improve care of children with terminal illnesses. Research that poses greater than minimal risk, and more than a minor increase over minimal risk, is allowable only if the research has the potential to directly benefit participants. This generally pertains to biomedical research with the potential to treat diseases or extend life expectancy.

Generally, the permission of at least one parent is required for a child to participate in research. The requirements for obtaining parental permission, as well as situations in which waivers can be obtained, are reviewed in Question #52. Children's capacity to understand the research and to give their informed assent for participation is discussed in Question #53.

Research conducted with children who are wards of the state must be either directly related to their status as wards or conducted in settings such as schools where most of the children are not wards. If a child who is considered a ward is to participate in any research, an advocate for the prospective participant must be appointed to provide permission, in addition to any individual who is acting as the child's guardian.

More questions? See #52, #53, and #57.

What Ethical Issues Should I Consider When Conducting Research With Individuals Who Have Experienced Traumatic Events?

Individuals who have experienced traumatic events such as abuse, rape, torture, war, domestic or community violence, disaster (natural or man-made), or forced emigration are often considered to be vulnerable by researchers, ethicists, and institutional review boards. This is due in large part to concerns about the potential for feelings of stress or distress to be reactivated during the research by remembering, analyzing, and discussing past experiences. It is also perceived that asking about traumatic events is more invasive than asking other types of questions, and that participants who have experienced trauma may be at risk of dignitary or social harm in the event of an unintended data breach.

Additionally, some behavioral research involves "challenge tasks," in which participants are exposed to reminders of trauma or they experience stressful social interactions through role-playing. Psychological assessments, standard batteries or tests, or biological assessments, such as the collection of blood or tissue samples to measure cortisol, are then conducted under these conditions. Theoretically, such research increases the potential for distress, including "retraumatization" of individuals who have experienced traumatic events. However, researchers believe these approaches can provide useful information about trauma, and these types of studies can be done ethically when appropriate participant protections are in place, such as monitoring and debriefing.

Despite these real concerns about psychological harm, some people may find participating in research to be a positive experience, even if they are asked questions about or revisit past traumatic events. Not only does such research provide an opportunity to tell one's story, but the potential to promote awareness of certain social problems or to contribute to the identification of potential solutions for prevention or treatment of victims can be empowering. However, some participants may end up being more upset than they had anticipated or even regret research participation.

Some participants may experience both positive and negative feelings about their participation in research.

If you are conducting research with individuals who have experienced trauma, you should also keep in mind that different people respond differently to stress. For example, many more individuals have been exposed to trauma than suffer from post-traumatic stress disorder (PTSD). There is no evidence that individuals who have experienced emotional or physical trauma have limited decision-making capacity due to the secondary effects of trauma, with the exception of individuals who may have experienced a traumatic brain injury.

You should also make it clear during the informed consent process that data collection is for research and not for treatment or therapy purposes. You should be especially sensitive to the potential for this misunderstanding when working with populations who lack access to services.

In research that may ask (or unintentionally learn) about child or elder abuse, consent forms must clearly state situations in which mandatory reporting laws require research staff members to report current or ongoing abuse. Participants should also be reminded throughout data collection to avoid using real names of people and places. Given the sensitivity of discussions and the public nature of some traumatic events (such as natural or manmade disasters), you should consider appropriate confidentiality protections, not just in data storage but also in reporting.

Self-care is important for any researcher who will be listening to, reading about, or analyzing data regarding the effects of traumatic experiences. This is especially true for researchers who are new to trauma research, such as students, for those conducting or reading transcripts from extremely personal interviews, and for those who have personally experienced trauma. Time to process what is being learned is critical; debriefing with a trained social worker or psychologist may be warranted.

More questions? See #16, #17, and #24.

What Ethical Issues Should I Consider When Conducting Research With Adults Who May Lack Decision-Making Capacity Due to Cognitive Impairment?

Individuals with cognitive impairment due to mental illness or developmental disability generally require special protections in research, but clear standards regarding appropriate protections do not exist.

People with cognitive impairments are potentially vulnerable in research due to their compromised ability to understand some or all of the information that is presented to them. However, the causes, effects, and permanence of cognitive impairments vary widely. Individuals with cognitive impairments are often lumped together in one group; but, in reality, each individual person—even among those who share diagnoses—is different. Individuals at risk for cognitive impairments may include individuals with schizophrenia and other psychiatric diagnoses, mild to severe developmental disability, dementia, Alzheimer's disease, or traumatic brain injury. Individuals in crisis may also temporarily suffer from cognitive impairment.

The decision-making capacity of individuals with certain kinds of diagnoses, in particular individuals with psychiatric illness, is often underestimated. The reality is that many different types of illnesses may affect decision-making capacity but the effects will vary among different people. Across any and all of these groups, diagnosis should not be the only factor in assessing decision-making capacity and ability to provide valid informed consent for research participation. Individuals may be harmed when their decision-making capacity is wrongly judged to be lacking. They may suffer dignitary harm or miss out on the opportunity to participate in research that may benefit them or future patients. It is a matter of ethics that researchers avoid overprotection. This may be especially prevalent in research with individuals with mild to moderate developmental disability. Even individuals who lack legal competence to consent to medical treatment or to manage their own finances may still have the ability to provide informed consent to participate in research, provided it poses no greater than minimal risk. For research that poses greater than minimal risk, a surrogate decision maker will likely be required.

Decision-making capacity may also change over time. Individuals with schizophrenia who are regularly taking their medications may be able to make independent decisions about research participation, but their understanding of the research or willingness to participate may change at times when they are not regularly taking their medications. The cognition of patients with dementia or Alzheimer's may fluctuate hourly, and may be particularly low at the end of the day (this is sometimes referred to as "sundowning"). In any research study, informed consent is an ongoing process and should be discussed at various time points in a study. This is especially true for individuals whose capacity may diminish as time goes on or whose capacity may fluctuate. In some situations, it may be appropriate to wait to invite someone to participate in research until capacity is regained, even if only temporarily.

Generally, individuals with cognitive impairments should be involved in research designed to provide future benefit to individuals with cognitive impairments. However, in some cases there may be a good reason for including individuals with a cognitive impairment in a study unrelated to their condition. For example, those individuals may share another, unrelated yet unique experience that is being researched; another diagnosis might make them eligible for a research study that may provide the prospect of a direct benefit; or a survey may seek to achieve broad community representation.

More questions? See #35, #47, and #48.

What Ethical Issues Should I Consider When Conducting Research With Students, Particularly Students Whom I Teach?

Teachers at the elementary, secondary, or university level may want to conduct research with their own students. For example, they may want to assess the effectiveness of a new teaching technique or better understand an issue, such as community violence, that affects a specific student population.

Exploitation is possible whenever a researcher and prospective participants have another relationship that exists within a hierarchical organization. Depending on the age of students and the type of institution, power relationships between students and teachers range from very subtle to extremely prescribed. Students may have difficulty saying "no" when approached by an instructor or teaching assistant. Some students may believe that saying "no" might harm their grade even if participation is not for credit, or believe that refusal may ruin their chances of getting a letter of recommendation. Even when appropriate protections are in place, it is important to realize that some individuals may agree to participate simply because they are eager to please. Enrolling students that you do not directly teach generally poses less of a threat to voluntariness and less risk to privacy and confidentiality than enrolling and gathering data from your own students.

Federal research regulations do not restrict the participation of students in research conducted by their instructors. However, many educational institutions have policies that limit participation of students with the aim of minimizing exploitation. Policies may prohibit researchers from requiring participation of students for course credit or offering academic incentives such as extra credit. However, in some situations, such as for university students, serving as a research participant can be a meaningful learning experience, especially for those who may one day become researchers. It may therefore be appropriate to offer course credit in exchange for study participation. If credit is offered, there should always be an option for an equivalent activity offering equivalent course credit; otherwise requiring research participation is coercive.

Institutional policies may also restrict the provision of financial incentives to students. Additionally, at some institutions, policies may limit the amount of research being done simply to minimize student burden or "research fatigue." However, policies may not be enough to protect prospective student-participants from the general pressure that they may feel when a teacher asks for a favor.

If students are younger than 18, parental permission may be required in addition to child assent (see Questions #52 and #53). Research conducted in elementary and secondary schools may also require the permission of the principal and/or additional review beyond that of the researchers' own institutional review board.

If you plan to conduct research with your own students, consider these ethical protections:

- Removing yourself from any consent and data collection procedures. For example, use a third party to obtain consent and collect the data. This prevents you from knowing which students declined participation.
- Restricting your access to the participant code list that links participant identities with their data. This provides an added layer of confidentiality to the data. However, such arrangements might not always be possible if the data collection requires personal interaction with you.

If you are conducting research on educational practices, it is also important to consider whether the research could adversely impact students' ability to learn or educators' assessment of students.

More questions? See #30, #49, and #53.

PART 5

OBTAINING INFORMED CONSENT

QUESTION #34

What Is Informed Consent?

Ethical principles dictate and federal research regulations require that before individuals can participate in research, they must give their permission—or their informed consent—to take part. Grounded in the ethical principle of "respect for persons," informed consent is designed to protect an individual's autonomy. That is, individuals have the right to say what can or cannot happen to them with respect to research.

The *Belmont Report* (1979; see Questions #3 and #4) describes three criteria that must be met for an individual's informed consent to participate in research to be valid. Prospective participants must

- be provided with sufficient information about the study (see Question #40);
- comprehend that information (see Questions #41 and #48); and
- voluntarily agree to participate in the research (see Question #49).

By providing their informed consent, participants affirm that they understand the purpose of the research and what it entails, and that their decision to participate was made voluntarily and free from coercion.

There are some exceptions. Federal research regulations outline certain circumstances when the requirement of obtaining participants' informed consent can be waived, or the informed consent process can be modified in some way. We describe these circumstances in Question #37.

More questions? See #35, #36, and #42.

What Is the Informed Consent Process?

Informed consent is not typically a one-time event when participants simply read and sign a consent form. Rather, it is a process that starts before prospective participants are given a consent form and continues until the end of the study. As a researcher, you want to ensure that individuals participating in your research understand it and what it entails, and give their informed consent to participate voluntarily without feeling pressured. You also want to ensure that participants continue to understand the study's purpose throughout study implementation. You must therefore determine what factors might influence prospective participants' decisions about participating in your study, such as information they learn during recruitment, and what steps are needed beyond the provision of written information for prospective participants to provide their voluntary informed consent.

For minimal risk studies with few study procedures, such as a one-time interview, you may be able to achieve the goals of voluntary informed consent just by having prospective participants read and sign the consent form or give their verbal consent after a brief explanation; study staff can be available for individuals who have questions. For other studies, such as those that pose more than minimal risk, simply having participants read and sign a consent form may not suffice. Additional mechanisms may be needed, such as allocating additional time for study staff members also to review the study with each prospective participant, ensure that all of the prospective participants' questions have been answered, and confirm that prospective participants understand the research—either formally or informally. For these reasons, obtaining informed consent from prospective participants is considered a process rather than just a signature on a consent form.

Extra consideration is needed for longitudinal research, where participants take part in multiple study procedures over time. Participants' understanding of the research may change as time goes by. Participants could, for example, begin to believe that the purpose of the research is to provide them with personal benefit rather than to provide the researcher with knowledge to help others in the future. Therefore, conversations about purpose, risks, benefits, and the right to stop participating at any time should continue throughout the course of the research. For research that poses more than minimal risk, ongoing assessments of participants' understanding may also be necessary.

More questions? See #36, #40, and #48.

What Is an
Informed Consent Form?

An informed consent form is a written document outlining a study's purpose, the research activities, and the risks and benefits of participation, as well as other key pieces of information. It is the primary way that researchers provide prospective participants with information about a study so they can make an informed decision about whether they want to participate.

Not all studies are required to use consent forms, even when some type of informed consent is required. Other questions address when participants must sign a consent form (Question #38), what information must be included in a consent form (Question #40), and how to write a consent form that is easy to understand (Question #41).

More questions? See #42, #44, and #80.

When Is Informed Consent Required?

Whether informed consent is required, and how it is obtained, varies depending on the risks of the research as well as the study population, setting, and data collection methods. For some studies, generally those that pose more than minimal risk, prospective participants must provide their written consent by signing the consent form before they can participate in the research. For other studies, including many that pose only minimal risk, prospective participants can provide their verbal consent instead of written consent (see Question #38 for a discussion of the differences between written and verbal consent). In some studies, participants' informed consent can be waived entirely.

Studies that pose no greater than minimal risk and are determined to be exempt from the federal research regulations (see Question #77) are also exempt from the requirement for informed consent. However, in exempt studies, prospective participants should still be told that their participation is voluntary and be provided with some key information (see Question #39). Exempt research does not require a waiver of informed consent or a waiver of documentation of informed consent from the institutional review board (IRB).

For research that is not exempt, the federal research regulations allow for informed consent to be *completely waived* in certain situations. If all the following conditions are met, an IRB may grant a waiver of informed consent (45 C.F.R. § 46.116 (c)(3)):

1. the research is minimal risk;

2. the research could not practicably be conducted unless a waiver was approved (and for research with identifiable data, the research could not be practically conducted without using the data in an identifiable format);

3. the waiver does not affect the rights of study participants; AND

4. participants are provided with information about the study after participation if appropriate.

Many types of social and behavioral science research studies meet these conditions, such as online surveys with large numbers of study participants, participant observations, and secondary analyses that do not otherwise qualify for exemption.

Whether research is exempt or qualifies for a waiver of informed consent, "implied consent" can also be used in research in the social and behavioral sciences, for example for paper-based or online surveys. In these situations, the researcher includes information typically found in a written consent form at the beginning of the survey, and an individual's informed consent is implied when he or she initiates the survey and answers its questions.

More questions? See #34, #35, and #36.

What Is the Difference Between Written and Verbal Informed Consent, and When Can Verbal Informed Consent Be Used?

When "written" informed consent is required, prospective participants sign a consent form, indicating their willingness to participate in the research. When "verbal" informed consent is allowed, prospective participants indicate their willingness to participate in the research aloud, but they do not sign a consent form. Verbal informed consent is a process that researchers use when the requirement for using written informed consent has been waived by an institutional review board (IRB).

According to the federal research regulations, the requirement to obtain *written* informed consent can be waived by an IRB in the following situations (45 C.F.R. § 46.117 (c)(1)):

1. the research poses only minimal risk and uses study procedures, such as surveys, that typically do not require written informed consent in nonresearch settings;

2. the research has no other records of participants' identities, making the signed informed consent form the only source linking the study participant to the research. In these situations, the signature on the consent form would be the main risk for potential harm if there was a breach in confidentiality; OR

3. the research is conducted among individuals who are not culturally accustomed to signing their names; the research must pose no greater than minimal risk and have other mechanisms in place to document informed consent.

For example, if you plan to conduct a single interview with individuals engaging in illegal behaviors (and will not collect participants' names for any purpose, such as scheduling), you may want to request a waiver of written documentation of informed consent and obtain verbal consent instead. If there was a breach in confidentiality, participants' names would therefore be unknown because you will have no documentation linking their names with their admission of engaging in illegal behavior.

Whether written or verbal informed consent is obtained, the same type of information should be provided to prospective participants. When verbal consent is used, researchers often use an information sheet, which looks like a written consent form, except there are no signature lines for the prospective participant and researcher to sign. Study staff members typically document the person's verbal consent in the study records, such as in a log or spreadsheet.

Informed consent, either written or verbal, can be obtained only after prospective participants have had information about the study explained to them; and they acknowledge that they have read (or heard) the information, understand the information, and are making a voluntary decision to participate.

More questions? See #36, #40, and #42.

What Are the Requirements for Informing Participants in Research That Is Determined to Be Exempt From the Federal Regulations?

While written or verbal informed consent is not required in exempt research, key information about the research should still be provided to prospective participants prior to initiating the research. Importantly, prospective participants should be told that their participation is voluntary. The type and amount of information that is provided may vary, as will the delivery format. This will depend on the research setting, population, and specific institutional review board guidelines, as well as researcher preferences. Typically, this information should include the requirements of the research (e.g., how long a survey will take), any risks and benefits, a statement regarding privacy and confidentiality protections, and, if applicable, any compensation the participant will receive. Information may be provided in writing (e.g., at the beginning of a survey, or in an information sheet) or verbally (e.g., before a telephone interview).

More questions? See #13, #37, and #77.

What Type of Information Must Be Included in an Informed Consent Form?

The federal research regulations (45 C.F.R. § 46.116 (a)(5)(i)) stipulate that consent forms must first concisely describe key information about the study that prospective participants will likely want to know to make an informed decision about participation before providing more detailed information about the research. The federal research regulations (45 C.F.R. § 46.116 (b)) also list the required information to include in informed consent forms:

- Describe that the prospective participant is being asked to participate in research. You should include information to differentiate the research activities from any services the prospective participants may currently receive at the same place that is conducting the research.
- State the purpose of the research. You should use lay language and nonscientific terms to describe what you are aiming to discover.
- Describe all the procedures that will be used in your research, painting a picture of what the individuals will experience if they decide to participate. This description should also indicate which procedures are experimental (such as whether the study will test the effectiveness of a new educational intervention) and whether participants will be randomly assigned to an intervention or control group. You should also indicate the time commitment required of participants (such as the hours spent completing surveys) and how long participation will last (e.g., at what point a longitudinal study will end).
- Describe all reasonably foreseeable risks or discomforts that may arise from participation (see Questions #11 and #12). Discussion of risks should not reflect the "worst case scenario" but rather focus on those risks that are most likely to occur and those that are likely important to an individual's decision about participating.

- Present the potential benefits of the research, including benefits to participants and benefits to others (see Question #14). You must take care not to overstate the potential benefits, particularly with experimental interventions as they do not yet have sufficient evidence of benefit (see Question #16).
- When applicable, describe any alternatives to participating in the research. This will apply only in research that is evaluating an intervention in some way. It must be clear to prospective participants whether they can receive the intervention or a similar intervention without participating in the research, or if participating in the research is the only way to receive this type of intervention. For example, if a psychology researcher is conducting a study to compare the effectiveness of two smoking cessation programs, the consent form should list smoking cession programs that are available outside of participating in the research, including whether the specific interventions offered in the research are available outside of the research. This helps participants to understand that research participation is not their only option.
- Describe the steps that you will take to protect the confidentiality of data collected during the research (see Question #23).
- Describe any financial compensation for research participation (see Questions #57 and #58). Compensation should not be presented as a benefit of research participation, but rather as an incentive or reimbursement for costs incurred (such as travel costs or time).
- Stress that research participation is voluntary (see Question #49). Prospective participants should be assured that they will not be penalized if they choose not to participate or if they stop participating after they are enrolled in the research. For example, individuals refusing or stopping participation should not lose any standard services provided by the institution where the research is being conducted.
- State whom participants can contact if they have questions about the research (usually the lead researcher) and if they have complaints, for example, if they feel they have been mistreated or misled in the research (usually the institutional review board [IRB] that provides oversight for the study). Names, telephone numbers, and emails of these individuals should be listed.
- Include one of two statements on the use of personal identifiers or identifiable biospecimens, if these are collected as part of the research:

a. that information and/or biospecimens collected in this research may be used by other researchers after all identifiers are removed; their additional consent would not be sought, or

b. that information and/or biospecimens collected in this research will not be used in other research, even if identifiers are removed.

The federal research regulations (45 C.F.R. § 46.116 (c)) describe that other information should be included if applicable, such as:

- the number of participants who will be involved in the study, if known, and
- a description of the circumstances under which an individual's participation may be terminated by the researcher. For example, it may be reasonable to state that people may be asked to leave a focus group discussion if they are rude or combative.

In certain circumstances, an IRB may approve the exclusion of one or more of the required elements from a consent form.

Additionally, most institutions have informed consent templates with required or suggested language that can be adapted to specific studies.

Researchers are ethically bound by the federal research regulations to be truthful in the information they present in consent forms and not to include any statements that appear to waive participants' legal rights (such as their right to sue the institution in the event of personal injury) or to release the investigator, institution, or research sponsor from liability (such as for negligence). Additionally, the informed consent form is often mistaken to be a legally binding contract because it includes technical and legal-sounding language, and participants are typically required to sign it. However, a consent form is not a legally binding contract. Participants are not required by law to comply with what they are asked to do in a consent form just because they have signed it, and they can stop participating in the research study at any time without penalties or other consequences. This is what makes a research consent form different from a legally binding contract.

More questions? See #36, #41, and #48.

How Do I Write a Consent Form That Is Easy to Understand?

A considerable amount of research has been conducted on how to write easy-to-read consent forms. While there is no gold standard, you should follow general principles. This includes using

- terms that are familiar to the study population;
- plain and simple language that avoids jargon;
- short sentences;
- shorter words ("take part" instead of "participate");
- active voice ("We will ask you questions about your health.");
- question and answer format ("What are the risks of taking part in the study?");
- short paragraphs, each focusing on a single concept;
- headers and subheaders to break up long sections;
- bulleted lists;
- "white space" so information is spread out on a page; and
- at least a 12-point font.

Many institutional review boards (IRBs) stipulate the reading level at which consent forms must be written. Often IRBs suggest an eighth-grade reading level or lower. You can use readability tools in word processing programs and on websites to check the reading level of consent forms. However, just because a readability software program determined that the consent form is written at a lower reading level, this does not necessarily mean that prospective participants will understand the information. Having individuals similar to those who will be asked to participate review the consent form and make suggestions on how to improve its readability and comprehension can be helpful.

Writing an easier-to-read consent form is just the first step in ensuring that prospective participants understand a research study. Allowing ample time for prospective participants to read the consent form, discuss its contents with study staff, and have all their questions answered satisfactorily must also be part of the broader informed consent process.

More questions? See #46, #47, and #48.

How Do I Obtain Informed Consent?

Processes to obtain informed consent vary. For example, for online survey research, prospective participants often read consent information online and proceed with completing the survey if they wish to do so, without ever speaking with study staff or signing a consent form. In face-to-face research where written consent is required, prospective participants often read the consent form, meet with a study staff member one-on-one to have their questions answered, and then sign the consent form if they wish to participate. Regardless of the type of study, however, three goals of informed consent—information disclosure, comprehension of the information, and voluntariness—must be met, as described in the *Belmont Report* (1979).

Information disclosure: Prospective participants typically learn about the details of a study through a consent form or information sheet. The type of information to disclose, regardless of the type of research, is discussed in Question #40. Depending on the study population and whether prospective participants meet face-to-face with study staff, study staff members should either read aloud the consent form or information sheet word-for-word to prospective participants or provide it to them with adequate time to read it themselves. In either situation, researchers should consider providing a verbal summary of what is written in the consent form or information sheet, highlighting key information such as risks and benefits.

Information comprehension: When prospective participants meet face-to-face with a study staff member, the informed consent process is an opportunity to discuss the study and to ensure that prospective participants understand the research and have had all their questions answered satisfactorily. Therefore, appropriate time should be allotted to obtain informed consent from each prospective participant. When prospective participants do not meet face-to-face with a study staff member, study contact information should be provided, and prospective participants should be encouraged to contact the study staff with any questions they may have; study staff members can also arrange telephone conversations with prospective participants, when appropriate. Additionally, informal and formal mechanisms can be used to assess prospective participants' understanding of the research prior to signing the consent form (see Question #48), regardless of whether consent is obtained in person or not.

Voluntariness: Decisions to participate in research must be free from coercion and undue influence. Prospective participants must make their own, voluntary decision about study participation (see Question #49). Study staff members should never attempt to persuade prospective participants to take part in research or provide their own opinions on whether the prospective participant should participate.

You must describe in your study protocol—and your institutional review board must approve—the specific process you will follow to fulfill these three ethical requirements and to obtain informed consent from prospective participants. Once participants sign a consent form (for written consent), give their verbal agreement (for verbal consent), or initiate research participation (for implied consent), they are now considered study participants.

Importantly, any designated study staff member responsible for obtaining informed consent must be sufficiently knowledgeable about the research so he or she can adequately answer all questions from prospective participants. Study staff members must also be comfortable reaching out to the principal investigator (PI) if they cannot answer a prospective participant's question—and the PI must make him- or herself available for any questions or issues that arise. Study staff should also receive training on facilitating the provision and discussion of the information in the informed consent form, and in obtaining prospective participants' signatures. This could include training on communication and adult learning principles, especially if the research study is complicated or poses significant risks. Study staff members may also need to practice obtaining informed consent from other study staff members or from mock participants.

Of note—for written consent, the study staff member who obtains participants' informed consent also signs the consent form. This signature documents that the consent form was read by or read to the prospective participant, that his or her questions were answered, and that the participant has given voluntary informed consent to participate in the research.

More questions? See #35, #43, and #44.

Who Can Consent to Research Participation?

Only the person who will participate in the research can give his or her consent to participate. Although prospective participants may choose to consult with friends and family about research participation, the ultimate decision is theirs and theirs alone. No one else can give consent on the behalf of the prospective participant or in place of the prospective participant's consent, unless the prospective participant does not have the legal authority to do so.

In research with adults who lack decision-making capacity due to a cognitive impairment such as dementia, a legally authorized representative may sign the consent form on behalf of an individual, depending on the situation and state law. For research with children, a parent or legal guardian typically signs a consent form for the child to participate. The child might also sign an assent form.

More questions? See #47, #52, and #53.

What Do I Do With the Consent Form After It Is Signed by a Participant?

Researchers must keep an original copy of all participants' signed consent forms. Additionally, federal research regulations require that study participants be provided with a copy of their signed consent form. Researchers may either (a) ask the prospective participant to sign two copies of the consent form and provide the participant with one of the signed copies, or (b) make a photocopy of the signed form and provide the participant with the photocopy. If participants do not want to keep a copy of their consent form, the researcher should document the participants' wishes.

Signed consent forms should be stored securely and plans for storage outlined in the research protocol. Importantly, signed consent forms should be stored separately from any study data because consent forms include participant names. This approach reduces the likelihood of a breach in confidentiality if an unauthorized individual accesses the study files.

You may also want to scan signed consent forms and store them electronically as backup to the paper forms. If this is done, appropriate confidentiality protections should be implemented, and original signed forms should not be destroyed until the study has been completed and the time required for storage has passed.

More questions? See #23, #36, and #42.

How Do I Obtain Informed Consent From a Prospective Participant Who Cannot Read the Consent Form?

The average American reads at an eighth-grade level, and a significant number of Americans have even poorer reading comprehension, or cannot read at all. Additionally, many individuals have vision problems and may not always have up-to-date corrective lenses. Therefore, you must prepare for instances in which individuals are not able to read the consent form or information sheet. Such individuals are still ethically and legally able to participate in research and should not be automatically excluded from research. Modifications to study implementation, such as having staff members read aloud the consent form, and surveys that were originally designed to be self-administered can be implemented to allow individuals with reading difficulties to participate. If research participation requires the ability to read, however, participants who cannot read can be ethically excluded.

If written informed consent is to be obtained from a prospective participant who cannot read the consent form, an impartial witness should be present. Impartial witnesses can be a family member or friend of the prospective participant or a patient advocate at a hospital, but they cannot be affiliated with the study in any way. The researcher typically reads the consent form aloud to the prospective participant, with the witness present. After all the prospective participant's and witness's questions have been answered, both the prospective participant and the witness sign the consent form. Prospective participants may sign with an X if they are unable to provide their signature. The impartial witness's signature indicates that the consent form was indeed read to the prospective participant, that the prospective participant had all her or his questions answered sufficiently, and that the prospective participant has made a voluntary decision to participate in the study. A witness is not typically required for verbal consent.

Researchers who anticipate having participants who are not able to read join their research should plan in advance for having an impartial witness regularly present. This process should be described in the study protocol, and an extra signature line should be included on consent forms.

More questions? See #41, #46, and #66.

How Do I Obtain Informed Consent From Prospective Participants Who Speak a Different Language From Mine?

If you will conduct research with individuals who speak a different language from yours and you must obtain written or verbal consent, the best process to follow for developing the consent form or information sheet is to have it written by someone who is fluent in the language of the study population and familiar with the details of study. For example, if you speak English and your study population speaks Spanish, someone on your team who speaks and writes in Spanish should draft the consent form in Spanish. Then, it should be translated into English by a separate person and reviewed by you to ensure that it correctly conveys the research study. This is the ideal process because the consent form is initially written in the language of the study participants versus being translated from another language.

In situations where study team members do not speak the study population's language fluently, it is acceptable to write the consent form or informational sheet yourself in English and then have someone else translate the document into Spanish. It is extremely important, however, to have the Spanish version of the consent form or information sheet then translated back into English by a person who was not involved in originally translating the document from English to Spanish to ensure that the meaning remained intact. "Back-translation" is a process in which a translator reviews the Spanish version of the document (without looking at the initial English version) and writes down everything that it says in English, creating another version of the document (the back-translated version). Then, you compare, section-by-section, the back-translated English version of the document with the initial English version of the document to see if they are consistent. The documents do not need to match word-for-word, but the meaning should be the same. If there are sections where the meaning between the two English documents differs, these can be noted and changes made to the Spanish version of the document; those sections should be back-translated into English again and reviewed to ensure correctness.

Both the Spanish and English versions of the consent forms or informational sheets should to be submitted to your institutional review board (IRB), so that IRB members who do not speak Spanish can review the document. The process of translation should also be thoroughly described in the protocol. Additionally, some IRBs may require documentation that certifies the Spanish and English consent forms convey the same information.

During the informed consent session, a person who speaks the language of the study population should obtain informed consent from prospective participants, when possible, so the study can be discussed and questions answered in the prospective participants' own language. If this is not possible, a professional translator should be present during the consenting process. Family members or friends of participants should not be used as informal translators.

More questions? See #54, #65, and #66.

How Can I Obtain Informed Consent From Individuals With Cognitive Impairments or Developmental Disabilities?

In most research that poses no more than minimal risk, individuals who have a cognitive impairment or developmental disability can provide informed consent for research participation on their own behalf, unless impairment is severe. However, if the research poses greater than minimal risk, informed consent must be obtained from the individual's legally authorized representative. In such cases, the prospective participant should be included in all discussions and his or her dissent respected.

State law determines who can consent to health care treatment on behalf of an individual who lacks decision-making capacity. Only a few states have laws that specifically address consent to *medical research,* and these may not apply in social and behavioral sciences research. Institutional review boards (IRBs) take varied approaches to determining who may serve as a "legally authorized representative" for the purposes of consent to a research study. Even if someone has a formal legal guardian, it might not be necessary—or respectful of autonomy—to have this person provide informed consent on behalf of an individual for a minimal risk social or behavioral research study that is relevant to an individual's condition. If you are conducting research with individuals with cognitive impairment or developmental disabilities, check your institutional guidelines.

Importantly, do not assume that individuals with a cognitive impairment or developmental disability cannot ever provide their own consent. Researchers must assess the capacity of each individual to understand the information about the study and to make an informed decision that is voluntary. It is important to note that for some conditions, prospective participants may have moments when they do have the capacity to provide their own consent and other moments when they do not. You must decide if it is appropriate to obtain informed consent during the moments of capacity, realizing that later when the participants take part in the study, their ability to understand the purpose of the study may have changed.

The process that you will use to determine capacity should be described in your study protocol. This will allow the IRB to better understand the capacity of the study population and how you plan to obtain their consent.

You should also take steps to make the consent form and process as clear as possible for all participants:

- Write the consent form to be short and easy to understand.
- Pretest the informed consent form with members of the study population or those who work directly with individuals in the study population.
- Informally assess prospective participants' comprehension of the research and continue the conversation about the study until adequate understanding is achieved. If it becomes apparent that consent cannot be obtained, either a legally authorized representative is needed, or the individual cannot participate. Utilize standardized tools for formally assessing decision-making capacity, such as the *MacArthur Competence Assessment Tool for Clinical Research*, in populations where some prospective participants may not be able to comprehend significant risks (Appelbaum & Grisso, 2001).

More questions? See #32, #41, and #48.

How Do I Know If a Prospective Participant Understands the Research?

In most social and behavioral sciences research, it may be sufficient to simply ask prospective participants if they understand the research. Or, even better, you can ask, "Tell me in your own words what the research is about." You can then clarify any misunderstandings. In research that poses considerable risk, is extremely complex, or includes individuals with cognitive impairment, you may want to assess comprehension formally and allow only those prospective participants found to have sufficient understanding to proceed with participation.

No gold standard exists for measuring prospective participants' understanding of research. Therefore, when a formal assessment is needed, you must decide what specifically prospective participants must understand about the research and how that understanding will be assessed.

Quantitative and qualitative questions, or a combination, can be used to formally assess prospective participants' comprehension of a research study. For example, a structured, multiple-choice quiz can assess prospective participants' understanding of key aspects of the study. When quizzes are used, researchers must decide the percentage of questions to be answered correctly in order for the prospective participant to enroll in the study. Researchers also must determine ahead of time whether any missed questions can be asked again after attempting to clarify the information with the prospective participant, and how many times the same question can be asked when answered incorrectly.

Qualitative assessments can also be used to formally assess prospective participants' understanding of the research. In these situations, study staff members ask prospective participants open-ended questions about the study. The prospective participants describe their answers to the questions, thereby demonstrating their understanding of the study. Study staff members then determine whether the prospective participants have sufficient understanding.

When formally assessing comprehension, researchers must describe whatever process will be used in their study protocol, so an institutional review board can determine whether it is sufficient.

More questions? See #41, #45, and #47.

How Do I Ensure That a Participant's Consent Is Voluntary?

Determining whether a prospective participant's consent is truly voluntary can be difficult. However, you can create an environment that encourages voluntary decision making. To do this, you must first understand the situations that may pressure individuals in the study population to agree to participate in research when they normally would not.

The *Belmont Report* (1979) provides useful guidance. It states that informed consent is considered voluntary when it is given in "conditions free of coercion and undue influence." Coercion occurs when someone purposely presents an overt threat of harm in order to obtain compliance from another person—for example, if prospective participants are told they will no longer have access to services they currently receive if they do not participate in a research study. Importantly, when research is conducted in a setting in which services are provided—or by the same person offering the services—prospective participants may *perceive* they will no longer have access to services if they do not participate in the research, even if this is never explicitly said by research staff members. Therefore, you must state in the consent form or information sheet and describe in discussions with prospective participants that service provision is not contingent on research participation. Additionally, informed consent should not be obtained by individuals who have authority or power over prospective participants. For example, supervisors should not be present or involved in the informed consent process for a study on employee satisfaction in the workplace. Otherwise, the prospective participants may feel they have no other choice but to join the study.

The *Belmont Report* explains that undue influence "occurs through an offer of an excessive, unwarranted, inappropriate or improper reward or other overture in order to obtain compliance." In other words, undue influence is often described as an offer too good to refuse. However, determining whether a particular incentive in a study leads to undue influence is difficult to do. For example, a researcher might offer prospective participants an incentive of $50 per study visit. Is this $50 incentive unduly influential? For individuals with steady employment, this amount of money may not influence their decision to participate. However, for individuals who are unemployed, this amount of money could influence their decision to participate in a study that they feel is too risky. Reasonable people will disagree on what amount of money constitutes undue inducement.

The *Belmont Report* also describes that undue influence includes attempts to persuade a prospective participant to take part in research for any reason. For example, a student who is a research assistant may not pressure her friends to participate in a study being conducted on campus just because she is responsible for enrolling study participants.

Ultimately, you should always stress with prospective participants that the decision about whether to participate in research is theirs alone. While it is completely acceptable for prospective participants to speak with and seek advice about research participation from their friends and family, it is not appropriate for someone else to force or otherwise try to convince them to participate. The final decision on whether to participate lies with the individual prospective participant. (For exceptions to this rule, see Questions #47 and #52 about research with individuals with cognitive impairments and children, respectively.)

More questions? See #27, #56, and #57.

Do I Need to Obtain Informed Consent Before Asking Screening Questions?

A sking screening questions prior to initiating the informed consent process is often necessary to determine the eligibility of prospective study participants. Those who are eligible then proceed with the informed consent process and enroll in the study if they wish. Those who are not eligible save time by not going through the informed consent process. For example, if a researcher wants to conduct a study with college students who frequently engage in binge drinking, screening questions could be asked to identify students who meet the researcher's definition of binge drinking. Then, only those students who are eligible—that is, binge drinkers—are invited to proceed with the informed consent process.

The federal regulations allow for screening questions to be asked without obtaining informed consent from the prospective participants, although the process must be approved by an institutional review board. Generally, researchers should not ask or retain identifying information obtained during the screening process without informed consent.

Before asking any screening questions, you should be very clear with prospective participants that the purpose of the questions is to determine their eligibility to participate in the research. Additionally, some information about the research should be explained to prospective participants to provide context for the screening question(s). Prospective participants should be told that if they are found eligible, they then will be provided with more detailed information about the research study and asked for their informed consent to participate.

More questions? See #37, #55, and #56.

Do I Need to Obtain Informed Consent From Individuals to Use Their Existing Data That Were Collected for Other Purposes?

When researchers answer a research question using data that were originally collected for another purpose, it is called "secondary data analysis." For example, a researcher collects food diaries from college students so he can identify the foods students eat weekly for breakfast, lunch, and dinner. Another researcher, who is not part of the original study, learns about these diaries and seeks permission to use those data to determine how often college students skip breakfast.

Secondary data analysis is considered exempt from the federal research regulations (and therefore does not require informed consent) when

- the existing data are de-identified (see Question #19) or anonymous (Question #20)—meaning that the data cannot be linked in any way back to the individual who provided the information (45 C.F.R. § 46.104(d)(4)(ii)); or
- the existing data are identifiable but the original study participants provided "broad consent"—meaning that participants agreed during the initial consent process for their identifiable information to be used for future unspecified research beyond the original study (45 C.F.R. § 46.116 (f)).
- the existing data are publicly available (45 C.F.R. § 46.104(d)(4)(i)).

In these situations, you would not need to obtain informed consent from the original study participants to conduct your secondary analysis. At most institutions, however, you will still need to submit your study protocol describing the secondary data analysis to your institutional review board (IRB) before beginning. If you are analyzing identifiable information, you should describe the procedures you are using to keep those data confidential.

If you are conducting a secondary analysis of existing data that include personal identifiers but broad consent was not obtained from the original participants, your analysis will likely not be exempt from federal research regulations. In these situations, you may request a waiver of informed consent from your IRB and describe why it would not be feasible to conduct your study if informed consent must be obtained; for example, because it would be impractical, if not impossible, to find all original study participants to obtain their consent. Information about how you will keep the data confidential during the secondary analysis must be described in your protocol that is submitted to your IRB.

You may also want to use a dataset for secondary analysis purposes that does not include personal identifiers; but the original researcher maintains a coded list of participant names, making it possible to identify individual participants. In these situations, if you will never have access to the coded list of participants names, your IRB may determine that the secondary data analysis is exempt from IRB review, and therefore consent would not be needed.

More questions? See #70, #75, and #77.

How Are Parents Involved in Decision Making About Their Children's Participation in Research?

Parents are entrusted with the legal responsibility for protecting their children, and therefore their permission is typically sought before a child can participate in research. Parental permission is the term used to describe when parents, or legal guardians, give their informed consent for their child to participate in research.

In research that requires parental permission, the process is similar to the informed consent process used with adults. Parents or guardians read, or have read to them, the parental permission form or information sheet. They are encouraged to ask questions and have them answered satisfactorily, and they must voluntarily give their permission for their child to participate in the research by signing the consent form or providing verbal agreement. With the exception of research that presents greater than minimal risk and no prospect of direct benefit, permission of one parent is usually sufficient to allow a child's research participation.

Some research with children is eligible for exemption, and in such cases parental permission is not required. In research that is not exempt, parental permission can be waived by an institutional review board (IRB) as long as procedures are in place to protect the child and the waiver is consistent with federal, state, and local laws. For example, an IRB may agree to waive parental permission in situations where the involvement of the parent/guardian could put the child at risk, such as with children who are neglected or abused, or among LGBTQ youth whose parents do not know or accept their child's sexual or gender identity. Waiving parental permission may also be possible when permission would be difficult or impossible to obtain, such as in research with homeless youth. Some researchers may also request to waive parental permission for research on sensitive topics, such as drug use. IRBs vary in their decisions regarding waivers of parental permission for research with children.

Parental permission may also be waived in situations where minors are legally "emancipated" and independent from their parents, such as in the case of marriage. Some state courts recognize the concept of the "mature minor," people under the age of 18 who are determined to be mature enough to make their own health care decisions independent of their parents. It is disputed whether mature minors are ethically allowed to enroll in research that poses greater than minimal risk and offers no prospect of direct benefit. Therefore, IRBs vary in their decisions regarding the inclusion of mature minors in such studies without parental permission.

More questions? See #30, #42, and #53.

What Type of Agreement Do I Need From Children So They Can Participate in Research?

"Informed assent" is the term used for a child's agreement to participate in research. If parental permission is needed—that is, the research is not exempt, and a waiver of informed consent has not been obtained—then you will need to consider obtaining some form of child assent, either written or verbal. The informed assent process involves (a) helping children to understand, at a developmentally appropriate level, the purpose of the research and what they can expect if they decide to participate, and (b) and soliciting their agreement to participate.

If you plan to conduct research with children, you must first determine the age of majority—that is, the age when individuals are considered adults—for that state or country (if determined at the country level) in which your research is to be conducted. In most states in the United States and many countries worldwide, individuals younger than 18 years of age are considered to be children or "minors." Informed *consent* to participate in research should be obtained from individuals at and above the age of majority; and informed *assent* should be obtained, with some caveats, from individuals under the age of majority, usually after obtaining parental permission.

The federal research regulations state that "adequate provisions" should be made for obtaining informed assent from children. Realizing that context matters, the regulations describe that "[i]n determining whether children are capable of assenting, the [institutional review board] IRB shall take into account the ages, maturity, and psychological state of the children involved" (45 C.F.R. § 46.408(a)). However, the regulations do not differentiate between very young children and older adolescents, so researchers must determine what is appropriate for prospective participants of various ages. Check your IRB's guidelines as they may have specific requirements for obtaining assent from children.

When it is appropriate to obtain informed assent from children, the process is similar to the informed consent process used with adults. An assent form or informational sheet is used, which may contain information similar to that found in informed consent forms. The form must be written at the appropriate developmental reading level, using plain and simple language. Children meet with study staff to discuss the study, review the assent form or informational sheet, and ask any questions they have about the research. In written informed consent, children sign the assent form to document that they have read (or have had read to them) the information in the assent form, that they understand the information, and that they voluntarily agree to participate in the study. Study staff members also sign to verify that the information about the study has been discussed with the child, that the child asked and had answered all her or his questions, and that the child voluntarily agrees to participate. Parents or guardians do not sign the assent form. Extra time may be needed for study staff to explain the research to children, making sure they understand the research and are able to ask and have answered any questions that they have about the research. If verbal rather than written informed consent is required, children simply state aloud their agreement to participate.

When a child's assent and their parent's permission are both necessary, you must determine whether a parent should be present when assent is obtained from the child. Consideration must be given to whether having a parent present may inappropriately influence children's decisions about research participation and infringe on their developing autonomy. On the other hand, some children may feel more comfortable with a parent present. Additionally, you must determine—and likely discuss with your IRB— how to address situations when parents want their child to participate in the research but the child does not want to, and vice versa.

More questions? See #30, #41, and #52.

How Should I Obtain Informed Consent From Prospective Participants When I'm Conducting Research Outside the United States?

The discussion of informed consent thus far has focused on the U.S. context and requirements. If you will conduct research outside the United States, you should first determine if the country in which you will be working has national regulations and guidelines on the conduct of human research, including the informed consent process. These must be followed. If your research is funded by the U.S. government, then the federal research regulations also apply and must be followed. The local regulations and the federal regulations may be in conflict, and ultimately the U.S. institutional review board (IRB) may decide that local regulations should prevail if they do not violate a person's autonomy.

You must also learn about the local research context and cultural norms and expectations. For example, how is individual autonomy viewed? What role do the community and family have in decision making? What is the study population's general understanding of research? How does the study population feel about signing a document? What language(s) should be used? What is the literacy level of the study population? What has been done in the past to obtain informed consent in other research studies?

In some cultures, it may be appropriate for the consent process to resemble the process typically used in research in the United States, primarily relying on a written consent form or information sheet. In other cultures, it may be necessary to design a very different consent process, for example, using flip charts with pictures and descriptions of familiar analogies to explain research concepts. Deciding on the best process to use often depends on the study population's education level and previous research experience, and on local expectations regarding informed consent.

Additionally, the process of obtaining informed consent, including the informed consent form if one is required, must be reviewed and approved by both a local ethics committee and the IRB at the researcher's institution.

Here are some guiding principles for obtaining consent from participants in a country different from your own:

1. Partner with a local researcher to develop and conduct the research, design the informed consent process, and write the informed consent form or informational sheet.

2. Find, read, and follow the local regulations and guidelines on research ethics and informed consent.

3. Obtain permissions from local leaders, if needed, to conduct the research within their jurisdictions. It is completely acceptable for researchers to ask a person in authority to give her or his permission to approach prospective participants in her or his jurisdiction, as long as this person and the prospective participants know that (a) prospective participants must decide on their own whether they want to participate in the research, (b) there will not be any consequences if prospective participants choose not to participate, and (c) the person in authority has no right to know who chooses to participate or not to participate in the research.

4. Identify the best way to explain the study in meaningful ways. Depending on the general literacy of the study population and prior research experience, consider culturally appropriate ways to explain the study, such as the use of familiar analogies, pictures, graphics, and drawings. A consent form may not be the best way to demonstrate respect for participants in cultures that do not typically use written documents.

5. Whether in writing or in conversation, be very clear about the purpose, risks, and benefits of research. Worldwide, people often have a difficult time understanding research, and some believe the purpose of the research is to benefit them personally.

6. Translate the consent form, informational sheet, and any other materials into the local language(s) and translate them back into English. Even better: write the consent form in the local language first.

7. Create a list of key research terms and translate them into the local language(s). Confirm translations with multiple people who speak the language. Use this list when translating the consent form if it is initially written in English.

8. Find out if signing the informed consent form is culturally appropriate for the study population. If not, identify an appropriate alternative, such as making their mark or thumbprint.

9. Obtain feedback on your proposed informed consent process and consent form from people in the study population and the local community. If necessary, create a community advisory board.

10. If culturally appropriate, offer to meet with spouses or other family members of prospective participants during the informed consent process to explain the study to them, if requested by the prospective participant.

11. Develop a culturally appropriate way of assessing comprehension of the study among prospective participants. For example, in some places, the use of a true/false quiz is not appropriate because prospective participants may find it difficult to disagree with a statement made by a study staff member, who may be viewed as having authority.

More questions? See #46, #65, and #66.

PART 6

DESIGNING ETHICAL RESEARCH

How Do I Ensure That Eligibility Criteria Are Appropriate and Fair?

Eligibility criteria for a research study consist of inclusion and exclusion requirements. Inclusion criteria are those characteristics that an individual must have in order to be eligible to participate in the research study. Exclusion criteria are characteristics that would prohibit participation. For example, a research study may require participants to be within a certain age range, such as from 18 to 25 years old. A study may require that participants have had a particular experience, such as growing up in a single-parent household; or have a particular health condition, such as diabetes. Additionally, a research study may exclude individuals with particular experiences or medical conditions. Exclusion may be based on the fact that participation would be too risky. For example, a research study of an exercise program with older adults may exclude those with heart conditions.

Exclusion may also be appropriate if there is good reason to believe that the experiences (and therefore the data) of individuals with certain characteristics will differ significantly from the experiences of a broader group—*and* there will not be enough individuals who share these characteristics (or enough resources) to make meaningful conclusions. For example, a small research study that aims to describe the college experience of hearing-impaired adolescents may reasonably exclude individuals who have other physical limitations.

In determining appropriate eligibility criteria, you must consider the scientific objectives of the research study as well as ethical principles, particularly the risk–benefit balance and justice. Research must be scientifically sound. If your eligibility criteria are too broad or too narrow, your ability to interpret and generalize your results may be limited. If your results are meaningless, then participants' time has been wasted, and they have possibly been subjected to risk for no good reason. Your inclusion and exclusion criteria must be justified in your research proposal. Importantly, inclusion and exclusion criteria should never be based on convenience. Eligibility criteria should be determined based on what is known about the phenomenon to be studied.

More questions? See #15, #27, and #50.

What Strategies Can
I Use to Ethically Recruit
People to Join My Research?

There is no one optimal recruitment strategy to recommend for all studies. Many studies require multiple strategies. The best strategies for a given study depend on the scientific aims as well as eligibility criteria, number of participants needed, time frame, and available resources. Be sure to check the recruitment policies of your institutional review board when you are developing your recruitment materials and approaches.

When recruiting for your study, you should protect individuals' privacy and avoid using approaches that will (1) identify an individual as being part of a specific group, (2) suggest that the individual engages in certain behaviors, or (3) give the impression that the individual has a specific condition. Protecting prospective participants' privacy is particularly important if the group, behaviors, or condition is stigmatized in any way.

Prospective participants may be approached through a variety of indirect or direct methods. Indirect methods include flyers; other types of announcements posted in public places; and radio, newspaper, television, or Internet advertisements that alert interested individuals to a study opportunity. Interested individuals call you, or your study staff members, to learn more about the research while choosing the amount of privacy they want when placing that call, such as calling from their home when they are alone. Methods that limit direct contact are most respectful of personal privacy but may not yield as many participants.

Direct recruitment methods include personalized letters, emails, telephone calls, and in-person requests. Direct methods may target individuals identified in a specific population. For example, in a community survey, phone numbers associated with addresses in certain zip codes may be randomly selected and called. Direct methods may also be used to reach those likely to meet eligibility requirements. For example, you may want to send letters to all parents of children participating in a school lunch program, with permission from school administrators. When using direct recruitment methods, you should explain to the prospective participants how they were identified and inform them that participation in research is voluntary. Although direct methods typically yield more participants, such solicitation may be considered by some to be an invasion of privacy.

Depending on the type of research study and the eligibility criteria, you may recruit at specific locations or sites. These may include schools, health care centers, organizations that deliver social services, businesses, and community centers or places where people who meet eligibility criteria are likely to be found. Direct or indirect means of recruitment may be used at such sites. Depending on the location, you may need to get permission from an authorized individual associated with the site. Health care institutions must follow HIPAA privacy laws (see Question #26) and may have additional specific privacy policies outlining guidelines for accessing patient records for research purposes. If individuals will be recruited in person—for example, at a community event—interactions should take place in a quiet, private location so that others cannot hear personal information being shared.

When recruiting for research through partner organizations, it is important that individuals who are approached about research participation understand and trust that refusal to participate will not compromise their relationship with the organization or affect the care or services they receive. If a partner organization's employees or volunteers will be involved in recruitment, these individuals must be appropriately trained regarding ethical standards for research. Partner organizations may have policies regarding sharing individuals' contact information with researchers, and researchers must respect these policies. It may be preferable for information about your research study to be sent directly from the partner organization.

There are pros and cons of having individuals from a partner organization make initial contact with prospective participants about research participation, rather than having the researcher make the initial contact. On one hand, the prospective participant may know and therefore feel more comfortable with an individual from the partner organization, such as a teacher or service provider. This may lead to better understanding of the research and a more valid informed consent. Also, given the organization's access to individuals who may meet the eligibility criteria, staff members at partner organizations can likely share information about your study with prospective participants one-on-one in a private place and provide information about how to enroll to those who are interested. Lastly, because the staff members are already informed of the prospective participant's health status or reasons he or she is obtaining the specific services, the individual's privacy is likely not violated (although some individuals may not like to be approached about research participation). On the other hand, the prospective participants may have a harder time saying "no" to someone they know.

Ideally, whoever approaches individuals about research participation should not be in a position of power over them. Concerns about potential undue inducement must be balanced with privacy considerations and the need for adequate informed consent. For example, a researcher should determine whether it is better to have employees at a social service agency invite their clients to complete a survey, or whether the agency should mail surveys directly to clients asking them to send it back to the researcher in a stamped, pre-addressed envelope. Each of these options has risks and benefits. Clients may feel pressure to participate because they are being asked by someone from whom they receive services. On the other hand, if the survey is mailed home, they will not have an opportunity to ask questions about the purpose and potential risks of the survey.

"Snowballing" is another recruitment approach. This is when participants identify people they know who they think will likely meet the eligibility criteria. When this approach is used, it is best for the participant to give the researcher's contact information to individuals rather than to give the researcher the individuals' names and contact information. That way, those who are interested can directly contact the researchers. It is a violation of individuals' privacy to give their information directly to researchers.

Many universities have subject pools that can be accessed to identify individuals meeting specific eligibility criteria. These pools will have guidelines regarding how participants can be identified and contacted.

More questions? See #57, #58, and #68.

When Is It Appropriate to Pay Participants for Taking Part in Research?

It is almost always ethically acceptable to offer some compensation, including monetary payment, to research participants. In some studies, offering money may be necessary to incentivize individuals to participate, especially if the research is particularly time-consuming or otherwise burdensome. For example, participants may be hesitant to enroll in research when research visits are frequent. Payment is not meant to offset the risks of the research, nor should it be presented as a benefit of the research. Rather, payment is considered reimbursement for participants' time, inconvenience, and transportation costs traveling to the research site or a "thank you" gesture recognizing participants' contribution. Small token items such as pens or tote bags are also appropriate incentives.

Researchers, ethicists, and institutional review board (IRB) members have expressed concerns that payment could lead some individuals to ignore research risks, thereby diminishing their ability to provide voluntary informed consent. This might happen if an individual decides to join a study because the amount of money provided is too high to turn down—an offer "too good to refuse."

Investigators can address concerns that compensation may be difficult to refuse by ensuring that the risks of any research study are appropriately minimized and communicated to prospective participants (an ethical requirement for all research), and that the payment amount is appropriate for the time and burdens associated with research procedures. The IRB will need to approve the incentive amount you plan to offer participants.

Some research institutions require that research participants provide personal information (and, in some cases, even Social Security numbers) in order to receive cash or check payments. This should be mentioned in the consent form as it increases the potential harms that may result from a data breach. It may also deter certain individuals from participating, including undocumented immigrants, other individuals who do not have Social Security numbers, or individuals concerned about identity theft. In lieu of cash or check payments, some studies compensate participants with gift cards. This practice is generally acceptable; but it may disadvantage certain individuals, such as those not able to easily reach a particular business to redeem their gift card.

For research with children, you can provide an incentive to the children, which could be a small payment or gift, if approved by your IRB. You should also consider whether payment should be provided to parents, as parents might incur costs, such as from transporting their children to and from a research clinic. The amount provided to parents should be appropriate to cover their costs, so as not to negatively influence parents' decisions about their children's participation. IRBs and organizations who work with children may have different policies regarding payments to children and/or their parents.

More questions? See #14, #56, and #58.

How Do I Determine the Appropriate Amount to Pay Research Participants?

Unfortunately, there is little guidance available to help researchers to determine suitable payment amounts. Few institutional review boards have established formal policies. Researchers at your university or in your department may have a general "rule of thumb" amount or range that they use. Some researchers multiply the local minimum wage by the estimated number of hours that will be spent in research participation. In reality, the range of payments offered varies greatly. If you are looking to recruit the same types of participants as other nearby researchers, it is important to recognize that researchers' prior payment practices influence participants' expectations, particularly if you are working in a heavily researched population.

Ethical considerations aside, ultimately, the amount that any researcher can pay participants will depend on the resources available and the costs of other research tasks, such as interviewer or data entry costs. It may be the case that using incentive payments can decrease other costs, such as the costs of recruitment materials or follow-up calls to schedule or reschedule research appointments. Payment to participants may therefore be a cost-effective means of achieving a sufficient sample size. In cases where the number of participants needed for a given study is quite high but budgets are small (or it's just not feasible to pay everyone), a lottery may be acceptable. In a lottery, participants who complete study requirements are entered with a certain chance to win a limited number of prizes (cash or other). The true chances of winning must be clear in the consent form or information sheet.

More questions? See #49, #56, and #57.

What Ethical Issues Should I Consider When Conducting Focus Group Discussions?

The primary ethical consideration in focus group research is whether gathering data in the group setting will pose greater risk to participants than conducting individual interviews. Risks to consider include informational risks (risks to privacy and confidentiality), social risks (risks to relationships), and emotional and psychological risks.

Collecting data in the presence of other participants limits your ability to completely protect participants' privacy and confidentiality, as you cannot control what participants share with others once the focus group is over. For this reason, you should inform prospective participants of this risk during the informed consent process. Additionally, you should consider the topics that will be covered during the group discussion. Research on any sensitive topic poses risks to participants' privacy and confidentiality as well as their personal comfort. Therefore, as a general rule, participants are not asked to discuss sensitive personal topics in focus groups. Rather, researchers use in-depth interviews to ask about topics that are likely to be sensitive.

Even when you do not plan to discuss sensitive topics, you should take steps to protect participants' privacy during focus groups, such as using first names only or pseudonyms. However, because the group meets face-to-face, even if participants do not reveal their real names, there is the potential for future recognition by the researcher and by other participants. Therefore, true anonymity is not possible and should never be promised. Even if you conduct focus groups over the telephone or online, participants may believe such forums are anonymous, but complete anonymity is not possible because all participants hear each other's voices.

It is common to audio record focus groups, transcribe the recordings, and analyze the transcripts; some researchers video record focus groups. Recording the discussion ensures the accuracy of data. However, recording poses potential additional risks to confidentiality; faces and voices can be recognizable, especially for individuals with unique voices because of accents or speech impediments. Any identifying information, such as the mention of specific places or people's names, should be redacted from transcripts during transcription. (See Questions #22 and #23 for best practices in maintaining privacy and confidentiality.)

Social risks are possible if there are preexisting or ongoing relationships among focus group participants. In the group setting, there is much more of a chance that potentially damaging personal information (for example, discussion of illegal behavior) or negative comments (for example, complaints about services) could get back to a third party (such as a service provider or an employer). What if, for example, in a focus group of recipients of state benefits, an individual discloses that she routinely lies on forms in order to keep her benefits? Even if confidentiality is promised by the researchers, another participant could share this information with a caseworker. If it is possible that focus group participants may disclose information that could be damaging if learned by a third party, it may be preferable to conduct individual interviews instead of focus groups.

Researchers use focus groups because when participants hear others' views and experiences, it may help them think differently or more deeply about an issue, resulting in more valuable comments from all participants. Focus group moderators should ensure a safe space for such sharing; but they must also be aware that participants may become upset by another focus group member's statements or when sharing their own personal experiences (which, as a general rule, is not the purpose of a focus group). Some participants may reveal more than they had intended to share. People sometimes feel more comfortable disclosing private, sensitive information to strangers than to friends or family. However, too much disclosure may lead them to become upset or to feel regret after the focus group. If a participant becomes upset, it may be difficult for researchers to notice because of the focus group setting. Depending on the research topic, referrals for local services or care may be needed for participants who become upset.

Several best practices can limit disruptions and ensure the comfort and safety of all participants. Before starting a focus group, tell participants that it is important that they demonstrate respect for others' views, talk only one at a time, wait to be called on, and do not talk about what was said in the focus group outside of the focus group. Focus group participants should be reminded that participation is voluntary, that they do not have to answer a particular question if they do not want to, and that they can stop participating and leave at any time. It should be made clear that their personal comfort takes precedence over their participation in the focus group at all times.

More questions? See #12, #17, and #100.

What Ethical Issues Should I Consider When Conducting Participant Observations?

Participant observation allows researchers to obtain data that may not be accessible through other data collection methods, such as interviews or surveys. Participant observation may involve brief observations of superficial activities or ethnographers embedding themselves in a community for several years. Each participant observation study is different; therefore it is difficult to apply ethical standards uniformly. However, people generally do not like to be "spied on," and some past research ethics scandals in social and behavioral science research involved observational research. In planning your observational research, consider the venue in which you will conduct your observations. What level of privacy do people in that venue generally expect?

If you are collecting data in a manner that does not allow for the identification of individual participants, your observational study will likely be considered exempt from federal research regulations oversight, and informed consent would not be required. For example, you might observe people's viewing behavior at an art museum and simply note numbers and basic demographics.

The more details you collect that could potentially make an individual identifiable—and the more private and sensitive the information you collect—the greater the risk posed by the research. If you must collect personally identifiable information as part of your observational research, written or verbal informed consent, or a request for a waiver of informed consent, may be necessary.

Another important ethical consideration is whether and when to reveal your identity as a researcher during the observation. This depends on the extent of the interaction between you and those you are observing. If the observation does not require you to interact with the participants, and you are not collecting any identifiable information, it is generally ethically acceptable for you not to reveal your identity as a researcher. However, if you are interacting with those you are observing, such as engaging in a conversation with them to elicit certain responses, you will likely need to obtain informed consent.

Covert observational research, in which a researcher spends an extended period of time in a particular setting pretending to play some role other than researcher, has raised many ethical objections. Those being studied have no knowledge that they are being studied. Covert research requires considerable ethical justification, given the overwhelming violation of the right to privacy. It can be justified only on the basis of the social benefit of the research. The scientific argument supporting covert observations is that individuals may change their behavior if they know they are being watched. However, there are important ethical considerations, such as the requirement of respect for persons in research, betrayal of public trust, potential harm to participants, exploitation of vulnerable individuals and groups, strain on the researchers of maintaining their cover, and the potential for harm if the researcher is discovered.

Covert observation that involves interacting with participants may be justified if the interaction is brief, and if the research data could not be collected in any other way. For example, you may want to pose as a customer at convenience stores to see if store clerks ask to see identification for the purchase of alcohol. Institutional review boards may have different views on the acceptability of studies like these, because of the potential for clerks to become upset for being observed without their knowledge— and potential harm to you, the researcher.

You may also intentionally or unintentionally observe illegal behavior during your research. If this is a possibility, you should plan in advance for how you will handle this, including whether your study will qualify for a Certificate of Confidentiality (see Question #25).

More questions? See #21, #37, and #72.

What Are Some of the Ethical Issues Raised by Deception in Research, and When Is It Ethically Acceptable to Use Deception?

Deception has been used in social science research since the early part of the 20th century. Ethical controversy erupted in the 1970s, after participants in the obedience studies of Stanley Milgram experienced psychological harm. Deception research has the potential to negatively impact public trust in research because, in general, people do not like to be deceived.

Deception in research can take different forms. Indirect deception occurs when the true purpose and goals of a study are not completely communicated to participants. In other cases, deception may be direct; for example, participants may be purposefully misled or given false information about an essential component of the study's procedures or given false feedback about their performance on certain tests or tasks.

According to the American Psychological Association's Code of Ethics, four conditions must be met in order for deception to be ethically acceptable:

1. **The study will make a significant contribution to scientific knowledge.** Participants may not be deceived in pursuit of answers to frivolous questions.

2. **The phenomenon of interest cannot be studied using other (nondeceptive) means.** Imagine you are seeking to study employment biases. You ask participants to evaluate potential job candidates who are identical on all qualifications but who differ by race, gender, and/or age. Alerting individuals to the purpose of the study will almost certainly influence their responses, as most people do not want to be perceived as being biased.

3. **The use of deception is not expected to cause significant harm or emotional distress to participants.** In deciding whether

to use deception in research, consider the type, probability, and magnitude of the potential risks of deception. Also consider the extent to which you are infringing on participants' autonomy by not giving them true or complete information. Deception may be considered an invasion of privacy because it may cause people to reveal things about themselves that they would prefer to keep private. If—such as in studies that involve false feedback—participants are led to believe something about themselves that is not true, this may be demeaning and have negative effects on self-esteem.

4. **Participants will be debriefed, and the deception will be explained as soon as possible.** Whenever direct deception is used in research, no matter how seemingly benign, a debriefing process is required. During the debriefing process, you should explain the true purpose of the study to participants; give them an opportunity to ask questions about the study; give them a chance to withdraw their data from analysis; and, if appropriate, assess them for any emotional distress or psychological harm, and provide them with appropriate resources. When deceptive measures are employed to elicit certain behaviors, participants should be reassured that their responses—for example, succumbing to the pressure to conform—are normal. Good debriefing can offset potential negative effects such as becoming upset or embarrassed.

More questions? See #7, #11, and #37.

What Ethical Issues Should I Consider If My Intervention Research Includes a Control Group?

In some studies, behavioral interventions or other social programs are evaluated to determine whether they are effective. Most scientists, including social and behavioral scientists, consider a randomized controlled trial (RCT) to be the gold standard for answering such research questions. In RCTs, some participants are randomly assigned to an intervention group and some participants are randomly assigned to a control group. Individuals in the intervention group receive the experimental intervention. Individuals in the control group do not receive the experimental intervention; they may receive the standard-of-care intervention, if one exists, or no intervention at all.

In a two-arm RCT, participants must understand that they have a chance of being randomized to a control group or to the unproven, experimental intervention group, and that being in either group carries different, unique risks. Therefore, consent forms—which are almost always required when a study includes randomization to an intervention, unless the intervention is brief and benign, such as playing a game—must adequately explain the various study arms and the chance of being randomized into one group or another.

If the experimental intervention is determined to be effective (for example, it improves educational achievement or prevents teen pregnancy), it may be ethically desirable to deliver the intervention to individuals initially assigned to the control group after the formal study period is over.

Conducting an RCT in a community-based setting poses unique challenges. Community members may want that intervention to continue after the formal study period is over if the research shows that it is effective. Funding may not be immediately available to continue the intervention—especially if policy change is required to provide that funding or to revise practice standards. Community research partners may become frustrated, feeling that benefits are being withheld from their communities. Researchers may be sympathetic yet lack the resources needed to help communities identify the funding to continue programs. This is an important ethical issue that should be discussed early on in any community–academic partnership.

More questions? See #15, #16, and #40.

What Ethical Issues Should
I Consider When Conducting
Research in a Defined Community?

Some research studies may involve a geographic community or a group of individuals who share a socially meaningful characteristic, such as race, ethnicity, disease status, or formal group membership. Examples of such groups include Appalachians, African-American women, people with diabetes, graduates of Harvard University, or children living on the West Side of Chicago. Because group membership may be easily determined, individual participants may be readily identifiable. Thus, participants in research conducted in a defined community may be more vulnerable to risk of disclosure of private information as well as the subsequent social harms.

When conducting research with a defined community, there are group-level risks as well as individual risks to consider. Group-level risks involve the potential for harm to all group members, regardless of individual research participation. Risks to nonparticipants include the potential for findings to stigmatize anyone who is a member of the community. For example, you may conduct a survey and find that Community A has a rate of self-reported prescription drug abuse that is 5 or 6 times higher than other surrounding communities. It is possible that upon learning this information, individuals from this community will be assumed by others—friends, family members, current or future employers—to be prescription drug abusers. This could result in social or economic harm to anyone who lives in Community A, not just to those who took the survey. The smaller the community is, and the more sensitive the data being collected are, the greater such risks.

Researchers must also consider the potential for research to pose risks to a community as a whole. In the 1990s, a geneticist working with an anthropologist collected blood samples from members of the Havasupai tribe in Arizona. There were fewer than 1,000 living tribe members at the time. The original purpose of the blood collection—as stated in the consent form—was to look for a genetic predisposition to diabetes. However, without either permission from tribal leaders or individual informed consent from participants, the researcher also conducted research on schizophrenia and shared samples with students and colleagues. One published analysis determined that the Havasupai's ancestors had migrated over the Bering Strait from Asia. This information contradicts the Havasupai's origin story, in which the original tribe members were from the base of the Grand Canyon. The publication of this information was potentially detrimental to group cohesion, as well as to individual tribe members' identities.

Given these potential risks, researchers conducting studies on a defined community must consider whether they have an obligation to engage members of that community in the design, conduct, analysis, and dissemination of the research. Arguably, the ethical obligation for such engagement is higher in defined communities because of the additional risks, as well as the potential benefits of community input on development and implementation.

More questions? See #11, #64, and #65.

What Is the Relationship Between Community Engagement and Research Ethics?

Traditionally, nonscientists have not been involved in the design or implementation of research studies or the interpretation of results. However, during the last few decades, academic researchers increasingly engage prospective participants and communities in planning and implementing research studies. Various forms of community engagement emerged in response to instances of abuse of research participants, out of recognition that research is often improved when communities are involved, and due to a perceived growth in "helicopter research"—in which researchers come into communities, collect data, and leave without informing them of the results. Although community engagement may not be possible or appropriate in all studies, and not all research topics or questions lend themselves to engagement, researchers should consider how the community could be involved when they begin thinking about a new research topic.

Community-based participatory research (CBPR) and participatory action research (PAR) are two specific approaches for engaging communities in the design and conduct of research, each with a defined history and literature. There are also many other approaches for involving prospective participants and communities in research development, implementation, and data interpretation. The umbrella term "community engagement" encompasses various strategies to involve nonresearchers who are stakeholders in the research results (often referred to as "community partners").

Different engagement methods are appropriate in different circumstances. Methods of community engagement may include

- holding open forums ("town hall meetings") to get broad, general input;
- establishing advisory boards to help design the research by giving input on specific issues and strategies;

- conducting formative research with prospective participants and members of their community to gather data to inform the research's study design and procedures;
- getting prior input on question wording from individuals similar to those who will take a survey, to increase validity of findings;
- hiring and training community members to serve as recruiters, data collectors, interviewers, and/or interventionists; and
- designating community leaders as co-investigators.

Community engagement in research has potential scientific, ethical, and community benefits. Engaging stakeholders in the identification and development of specific research questions and agendas can ensure that issues that are important to communities are studied and increase the real-world utility of results. Community engagement may lead to better data, which in turn should lead to improved community health. Community engagement may also improve enrollment and response rates. For example, engaging known, trusted community organizations in recruitment efforts can encourage participation and, perhaps, lead to faster enrollment, saving time and money.

Community engagement can also enhance the ethics of research by increasing transparency between researchers and communities, improving the informed consent process, and identifying individual- and community-level risks and ways to minimize those risks. Meaningful community engagement can also develop community capacity to conduct research and apply results.

Determining whether and to what extent you might engage communities in your research depends on many factors. Community engagement first and foremost can be thought of as a philosophical or ideological commitment to respecting the expertise of nonscientists, to building community capacity, and to advocating for change. Although involving communities is likely important for many kinds of research, if you plan to conduct research with a disenfranchised community, or suspect that your research may impact a defined community, you should consider engaging the community. If you are conducting research with populations who are hard to reach or are particularly suspicious of research due to past bad experiences, community engagement is also likely necessary. You may be able to partner with existing community organizations to conduct your research, or you may need to identify informal community leaders and representatives and bring them together. Keep in mind that those people who best represent the "community" may not always be readily identifiable, enthusiastic about research, or able to dedicate the necessary hours. Importantly, researchers should engage with the community early in the planning process so that there is time to adequately incorporate community input.

Advocates of community engagement argue that involving communities makes research more ethical. Although community engagement does demonstrate respect for a community and its values, and it may remedy some of the problems that arise when conducting research within communities, community engagement is not without its own ethical challenges. Researchers are not used to sharing decision making or data ownership, therefore, these negotiations may be challenging. Community partners may perceive researchers as speaking a different language, which may hamstring even the most well-intentioned efforts at genuine engagement and power sharing. Community partners, particularly advocacy groups, may have very different goals than academic researchers, complicating shared decision making. Expectations regarding research risks, efforts to minimize risks, and the potential for individual- and community-level benefits must be clearly defined before research begins.

Community engagement in research may also pose specific risks to research participants. When someone is invited to participate in research by people they know or on whom they depend for services, this may threaten their voluntary participation and the informed consent process. Problems with data integrity may also arise if those responsible for data collection are not trained in scientific methodology, have ideological conflicts of interest, or do not have adequate power in their roles—for example, if they fear they might be fired if they do not recruit enough participants. Community partners who are responsible for data collection or intervention delivery may experience distress, for example, when they are not able to offer an intervention they feel is beneficial to someone randomized to the control group.

When engaging community members in research, it is important for researchers to demonstrate respect for the expertise that they bring to the table. Be genuine in your efforts to listen to community input and incorporate that input into your research plan. Expect to hear things that may challenge your assumptions about the topic you are studying.

Community partners who have responsibilities for research design and/or data collection and analysis—whether they are formally employed by your institution or not—will need to complete research ethics training if they will interact with study participants and/or their data. It is important that all community partners, regardless of their specific role, understand the foundational ethical principles of research.

More questions? See #27, #63, and #65.

What Does Cultural Competence Mean, and How Do I Apply It to Research Ethics?

Simply put, cultural competence involves demonstrating respect for differences. In the context of research ethics, cultural competence requires that researchers do not blindly apply ethical principles to research conducted in cultures that may have different interpretations of respect, benefit, or justice.

For example, in the United States, a country founded on an ideal of independence, autonomy means something very specific. In research, this translates to individual informed consent, often utilizing a formal signed document. Conceptions of autonomy may vary worldwide as may the comfort level with signing documents. As a result, the informed consent process may need to be altered in order to demonstrate respect for participants in a different culture. Although the ultimate decision about research participation should lie with the participants themselves, community and family have a significant role in decision making in many cultures. Additionally, the concept of individual consent or signing documents may be unfamiliar. In such cultures, favoring privacy over communal decision making, or requiring individuals to sign documents does not respect their autonomy and does nothing to protect their rights.

How do you ensure that you are being culturally competent in conducting your research? Partner with local researchers. Ask questions about cultural norms and expectations. Listen and learn from your partners. Understand that different cultures also have distinctive norms regarding privacy, confidentiality, and modesty. These must be respected in research, while still adhering to standard ethical principles and relevant research regulations. For example, having a male research assistant ask female participants questions about reproductive health matters may be perceived as extremely disrespectful, and may even be traumatic for research participants from certain cultures.

Use participants' preferred language, but keep in mind that language is about more than just translating materials for non-English speakers. All research documents—flyers, consent forms, surveys and other instruments, intervention materials—should reflect how the people you are trying to reach think, talk, look, and act. Photos, examples, and vocabulary can affect enrollment rates, the completeness and accuracy of responses, and—most importantly—participants' comfort.

Communication also includes nonverbal cues, such as body language. Different actions carry different meanings in different cultures. For example, direct eye contact may be used as a sign of respect or attentiveness, or it may be completely avoided out of a desire to show respect.

Much has been written about the benefits of having culturally matched research team members. However, cultural competence or congruence cannot be assumed just because of the way someone looks. Proficiency in a foreign language does not equate to cultural competence.

Truly becoming culturally competent takes time and effort. The best way to learn about a culture is to ask people to share their culture with you. Cultural competence cannot be learned by reading a book. It requires active engagement and humility. When working in unfamiliar cultures, collaborating with community partners who can share information about the cultural norms of prospective participants will be necessary. In some cases, formative research prior to full implementation may be required in order to determine the most culturally appropriate research methods, strategies, and communications. Carefully listening and observing will go a long way in helping you demonstrate cultural competence.

More questions? See #46, #54, and #66.

What Ethical Guidelines and Regulations Should I Consider When Conducting Research in Another Country?

United States researchers conducting research in other countries are generally bound by U.S. regulations as well as the regulations of the country in which they are working. Often this means that research must prospectively be reviewed by both a U.S. institutional review board (IRB) and an ethics review board in-country, if the other country has such a mechanism for research oversight. Consult with your institution's IRB as soon as possible to ensure a timely and appropriate review. Your collaborators should be familiar with the process at their own institutions.

As a researcher, it is your responsibility to know the rules and regulations of the country in which you are working. The U.S. Office of Human Research Protections (OHRP) also compiles a list of international and country-specific laws, regulations, and guidelines related to human research, available on the OHRP website. Several guidance documents also exist to inform the ethical conduct of research from an international perspective. Many are available online.

Different countries may have different standards regarding issues such as privacy protections or informed consent procedures. It may not be obvious how to adhere to both, or which standard supersedes which, for a particular issue. Determining how to develop recruitment strategies, consent processes, and confidentiality protections that satisfy the standards of both or all countries in which you are conducting research will require early and ongoing discussion with your local collaborators, as well as with all IRBs that will be reviewing your research.

More questions? See #46, #54, and #76.

PART 7

ADDRESSING ETHICAL ISSUES IN ONLINE RESEARCH

Are There Specific Ethical Guidelines for Conducting Research Online?

The popularity of the Internet and the ubiquity of mobile devices provide an extraordinary number of opportunities to engage more people in research and to collect data in new ways. The Internet enhances how research can be conducted, yet numerous questions have been raised about how ethical principles should be followed when using the Internet for research purposes. While researchers must follow the federal research regulations when conducting research online, the regulations do not specifically address the unique ethical issues that arise when conducting research using the Internet. To address these challenges, some guidance, including codes of ethics, are available. Additionally, many institutions have developed their own guidelines for online research. While it is unfeasible, in this book, to cover all the possible scenarios when conducting research using the Internet, we highlight several important ethical aspects to consider when designing your online research.

More questions? See #68–#73.

What Ethical Issues Should I Consider When Recruiting Study Participants Online?

Researchers commonly use the Internet to recruit study participants, whether the study will be conducted online, over the phone, or in person. Researchers are no longer limited to hanging recruitment fliers on walls and bulletin boards, hoping that people who meet the eligibility criteria will see a flyer and call the posted telephone number to enroll. Researchers can advertise their research on social networking websites, organizational forums, listservs, and blogs, for example. Although these approaches still rely on people taking some action to join the study, such as visiting the study's website or calling study staff to enroll, online recruitment has the potential to reach many more eligible and interested participants than traditional recruitment approaches. Regardless of whether you post information about a research study online or via a flier on a billboard, the same type of information is ethically required. In addition, all recruitment materials must be reviewed and approved by an institutional review board before they can be used.

Recruiting using the Internet poses particular challenges when you will never meet participants face-to-face. For example, you may send recruitment emails to prospective participants that include a direct link to an online survey. It will be very challenging for you to verify the ages and other eligibility criteria of the individuals who click on the direct link. Therefore, an important step in enrolling an eligible population is to focus your recruitment efforts toward individuals who are likely to meet the eligibility criteria. For research with adults, this means (1) posting recruitment information on websites typically visited by adults, and not by children, and (2) making the age criterion very explicit. For some studies, you also may need to put into place specific procedures to verify the participants' ages before they are enrolled. To limit the likelihood of enrolling ineligible participants, some researchers choose to recruit via the Internet, and possibly even to collect data online, but speak with interested individuals either face-to-face or over the telephone to confirm eligibility and obtain informed consent before enrolling them.

For some studies, you can best reach your study population through private listservs or websites. For example, if you are interested in interviewing individuals with asthma, the most targeted recruitment approach might be to partner with an organization that supports individuals with asthma and to send out an announcement on their private listserv or post information on the organization's website. In these cases, permission must first be sought by the owner of the listserv or website. Additionally, information about which members participate must be kept confidential and not shared with the owner of the listserv or website.

More questions? See #55, #56, and #73.

What Ethical Issues Should I Consider When Collecting *New* Data Online?

Online survey applications that can be accessed via computers and mobile phones are commonly used in research. Collecting data using these technologies allows you to gather data at times and in places that are convenient for study participants.

Three main ethical issues should be considered when collecting new data online. First, researchers must ensure that the study participants meet all eligibility criteria, including age criteria. Second, researchers must ensure that they appropriately obtain informed consent.

Third, researchers must put procedures in place to protect participants' privacy and the confidentiality of their data. Keep in mind that it may be very difficult to collect anonymous data using the Internet, even if Internet Protocol (IP) addresses are not collected. An individual's footprint on the Internet might make it possible to identify him or her. If you collect certain kinds of information, participants could possibility be identified if someone has the time and resources to put together pieces of information from the research summary and information available from multiple Internet sites that the participants use.

To limit the likelihood of a data breach or of others' learning participants' identities in online research: (1) ask only information that is necessary to know to answer your research question, (2) learn as much as you can about the particular online research software platform you plan to use so that you can understand its unique benefits and pitfalls, (3) check with the software company to determine whether it is possible to record responses without recording IP addresses and other possibly identifiable information in the software's background, and (4) be rigorous in your privacy and confidentiality procedures. Whenever possible, use resources offered by your university, such as online survey software; these will have been previously vetted for certain features and may include additional security protections, such as automatically storing data behind a firewall. Additionally, when using an online research software platform, find out how the data are being stored (e.g., are the data encrypted?), who might have access to the data (e.g., employees at the software company?), and if and how data can eventually be permanently deleted from the online database. Contact staff at the software company to get answers to these questions.

Similarly, when using a mobile phone app to collect data, be sure you understand the app's privacy and confidentiality features by asking questions, such as the following:

1. Are data stored on the mobile phone or automatically transmitted to an online server and deleted from the phone? If data are stored on the phone, will the phone be password-protected? If data are stored on an online server, are the data encrypted when being transmitted from the phone? How are they securely stored on the server?

2. Will staff of the data collection app or others have access to data that are collected using that app? Will they use the data for other purposes?

More questions? See #23, #70, and #71.

What Ethical Issues Should I Consider When Using Data That Already *Exist* Online?

Researchers often use information that already exists on the Internet to answer research questions. The Internet provides a wealth of existing information that can be easily accessed. Throughout the day, people share their thoughts, concerns, experiences, and aspirations in chat rooms, in blogs, and on social media.

Even though most information that exists on the Internet is considered public and is accessible, you must consider several issues before using it for your research. First, consider the rules of the site where the information is posted. When individuals post information on the Internet—*even information that they feel is private*—it is typically considered public unless the privacy policy of the site where it is posted expressly states otherwise. Researchers, just like anyone else, must follow whatever rules are stated in the privacy policy. If there is no statement on the website that the contents should be considered private, you may be able to use this information for research purposes.

Second, you should also be mindful of the privacy *expectations* of users of the site, regardless of the privacy policy (or lack of one). Just because the information is considered public doesn't necessarily mean that you *should* access it and use it in your research. Ask yourself: What is the privacy norm or expectation established for the site? What is the privacy expectation, given the topic under discussion? Meaning, are people providing information that they expect will be seen only by people similar to them, or is the expectation that anyone on the Internet can easily access this information? Is the information sensitive or deeply personal in any way, or does the information focus on a mundane topic? For example, individuals likely have the expectation that anything they share via Twitter is considered public information. However, individuals likely expect that information shared through a moderated, online chat group will not be communicated outside of that group.

Third, you must also plan for protecting people's privacy and the confidentiality of their data once collected from existing Internet sites. Often information provided on the Internet is identifiable or can be identifiable. Some people who use social media use their real names when posting information while others use pseudonyms that may be traceable to a real identity. Even in situations where only first names are used, or when people choose to use pseudonyms, other information is often posted that can be used to identify the person. While you may be allowed to access public information on the Internet for research purposes, you still must have procedures in place to protect people's privacy and to limit any breaches of confidentiality of information once it is compiled for research purposes. Importantly, do not include any identifiable information when reporting research findings.

Depending on the type of existing data used, an institutional review board (IRB) may determine the research to be exempt from federal research regulations. In some situations, however, you may need to request a waiver of written (signed) informed consent from the IRB to use the data, or you may even need to obtain informed consent from the people who provided the information online. IRBs will likely vary in their determination.

More questions? See #21, #60, and #72.

How Do I Document Informed Consent When Conducting Research Online— and Ensure That Participants Understand the Research?

For research that has been determined to be *exempt* from ongoing oversight by your institutional review board (IRB), participants do not need to provide their written or verbal consent to participate in the research. This will apply to many online surveys or other research activities such as online focus groups. However, it is still a good practice to provide some information about a study at the beginning of the online survey or focus group, such as the purpose of the study; how long the survey will take; risks and benefits; procedures to protect privacy and confidentiality; and the name, phone number, and email address of someone the participants can contact with questions.

For online studies that require informed consent, multiple approaches can be used to document consent. If your IRB has waived written (signed) consent, you may be able to obtain implied consent. In these situations, for example, you can state at the end of the introduction section of the online survey: "By starting the survey, I am giving my informed consent to participate in the research." Individuals who wish to participate proceed with completing the survey, and uninterested individuals do not. Another approach to document consent when written (signed) consent is waived is for participants to check a box indicating their agreement to participate. At the beginning of the online survey, participants can be asked: "Do you agree to participate?" Individuals who wish to participate click an "I agree" button to proceed with the survey, and those who don't want to participant click an "I disagree" button.

When written informed consent is required, participants may be able to provide an electronic signature to document their consent. In some situations, you may need to meet with prospective participants face-to-face for the initial study visit so they can provide their actual signature on an informed consent form. All follow-up data could then be collected online.

For some studies, you may want to confirm or assess participants' comprehension of the research before they can proceed with their participation. If you are conducting an online survey on a nonsensitive research topic, for example, you could require prospective participants to click on a button that reads "I understand and agree to participate in the research" after reading information about the study, but before proceeding with the online survey. For some studies, you may want participants to correctly answer quiz questions about the study before they can proceed to an online survey. If individuals do not answer a certain percentage of the questions correctly, they cannot proceed with taking part in the research. Researchers should always include a phone number or email address of study staff so prospective participants can obtain answers to any questions they have about the research before participating.

More questions? See #37, #39, and #40.

Is It Ethical for Me to Join an Online Discussion Group or Chat Room for Research Purposes Without Informing the Group That I'm a Researcher?

If you join an online group (public or private) or chat room and ask questions and/or contribute to the discussions, that interaction may be considered research. In addition to the institutional review board (IRB), approval from the chat room organizer will also likely be necessary. Depending on the written guidelines as well as unwritten expectations of group members, members may need to be informed that a researcher is participating and asking questions for research purposes, as conducting research without informing members may violate the norms of the group. In cases that pose risks to members' privacy and confidentiality, or when identifiable information will be collected, informed consent may be required.

For some research, you may need to only view a public chat room discussion but not interact with other members of the group (that is, you don't post anything, but rather just look at what others have posted). In these situations, you should consider the type of discussion group and information shared. For example, people who share information in a chat room for survivors of domestic violence may likely have an expectation that the other people in the chat room are also survivors of domestic violence. It's reasonable to think that they may become upset upon learning that their information was used for research purposes without their knowledge. In comparison, people may share information in another chat room regarding their feelings about watching TV but will not be concerned that researchers use their information—as the topic is neither sensitive nor very personal to them. Depending on the topic, you may have an ethical duty to alert members that you are using their information for research purposes or to obtain permission from the group moderator and individual members.

Determining how to best approach research in online forums in an ethical manner is not always easy. Consult advisors, colleagues, and your IRB for guidance or assistance in thinking through what level of engagement with online discussion groups is ethical and whether moderators' permission or members' informed consent is needed.

More questions? See #21, #60, and #63.

How Do I Verify the Age of Individuals Who Participate in My Online Research?

Conducting research exclusively online makes age verification tricky. Because there are no in-person study activities where researchers can visually confirm age or ask for an official identification card, if necessary, it may be difficult for researchers to truly know the ages of individuals who participate in their research. Therefore, you may never be able to verify participants' ages. However, there are a few steps that you can take to increase the likelihood that you enroll only individuals who meet the age eligibility criterion:

1. Advertise your research on Internet sites that are frequented by individuals who match your age eligibility criterion.

2. Provide clear instructions on the age eligibility criterion: "You can participate in this research only if you are 18 years of age or older."

3. Have individuals enter their year of birth before they are allowed to proceed with the survey; those who do not meet the age eligibility criterion cannot proceed with the survey.

4. Use an online age verification system; several are available online, although they are far from failproof.

More questions? See #68.

PART 8

NEGOTIATING THE IRB REVIEW PROCESS

What Is an IRB, and
Who Are the Members?

An institutional review board (IRB) is the committee at your institution responsible for prospectively reviewing research that involves human participants and applying federal research guidelines and institutional polices to ensure that research is conducted safely and ethically. Research that poses greater than minimal risk will be reviewed by the full board at a convened meeting. Research that poses no greater than minimal risk and qualifies for either exemption or expedited review will be reviewed by one or two IRB members as designated by the IRB chairperson.

According to federal research regulations, an IRB must consist of at least five members with different expertise. At least one member must be a scientist, at least one member must be a nonscientist, and at least one member must be not otherwise affiliated with the institution; most members are scientists at the institution. One member is designated as the chairperson; there may also be a co- or vice-chairperson. Most IRBs include many more than five members—usually between 15 and 25 members, depending on the size of the institution as well as the number of IRBs at that institution. Many institutions have more than one IRB.

IRBs also must be diverse in terms of race and ethnicity, gender, cultural background, and scientific expertise. If no board member has the specific expertise that is required to review a particular protocol, such as knowledge about a specific method or vulnerable population, an IRB may ask someone who is not a member to act as an ad hoc reviewer.

Federal research regulations do not specify qualifications for a nonscientist IRB member. Any nonemployee living and/or working in the community where research is being conducted and from where participants are drawn may serve as a nonaffiliated IRB member. Many IRBs include one individual who is both nonscientific and nonaffiliated in order to meet the requirements. This individual is sometimes referred to as a "community member." These individuals may be former research participants, patient advocates, clergy members, lawyers, teachers, or homemakers. The ideal nonscientist member is someone who is familiar with the local community, cognizant of the potential for exploitation of disadvantaged groups, willing to read lengthy documents and attend long meetings, and capable of presenting his or her viewpoint in a large group that may be full of opinionated scientists.

If an IRB reviews research conducted with prisoners, there must also be a prisoner representative. This may be a current or former warden, prison chaplain, or other prison employee, prison advocate, or former prisoner. Prisoner representatives should not review research that will be conducted at any facility where they are currently employed.

Conflicts of interest must be avoided in IRB review. No member is allowed to review or vote on a protocol in which he or she is involved as an investigator, advisor, or consultant.

In addition to the IRB members, most IRBs are staffed by professionals who help to run the day-to-day activities of the IRB, such as managing correspondence with researchers. IRB staff members may also conduct reviews of minimal risk research that does not need to be reviewed by the full board, such as research qualifying for expedited review (see Questions #78 and #79) or exemption (see Question #77).

Research ethics boards outside of the United States have different membership requirements. Some include more nonscientists and may require inclusion of specific nonscientific professionals, such as lawyers, members of the clergy, or ethicists.

More questions? See #9, #75, and #76.

How Do I Know If My Study Must Be Reviewed by an IRB?

If you will be gathering information from or about people, you will need to consider whether your proposed activities must be reviewed by an IRB. The need for IRB review depends on whether what you are proposing meets the criteria of two very specific regulatory definitions—the definition of "research" and the definition of "human subject" (how the federal research regulations refer to what we prefer to call a "research participant").

While it is reasonable to think that any activity that gathers information from people by researchers is research with human subjects, there are some exceptions according to the federal research regulations. Ultimately, however, your IRB—not you—decides whether your proposed activities need IRB review and, if so, the type of review. This means that even when you think your proposed activities do not meet the definition of "human subjects research," you must consult with your IRB to confirm. Some IRBs have formal processes for this.

The federal research regulations include definitions of both "research" and "human subjects." IRBs used these definitions to determine which proposed activities require their review. First, the IRB will determine whether the activity you are planning is, in fact, considered research, defined as "a systematic investigation, including research development, testing, and evaluation, designed to develop or contribute to generalizable knowledge" (45 C.F.R. § 46.102(l)). This formal language is a bit difficult to interpret. Think of it this way: If you are trying to learn something new about a social phenomenon; and you are going about it in a logical, methodological way; and you plan to share your results with others so that they can build on them in future research, then you are conducting research.

The IRB will also consider whether your proposed activities involve human subjects, defined as "living individual[s] about whom an investigator (whether professional or student) conducting research: (i) Obtains information or biospecimens through intervention or interaction with the individual, and uses, studies, or analyzes the information or biospecimens; or (ii) Obtains, uses, studies, analyzes, or generates identifiable private information or identifiable biospecimens" (45 C.F.R. § 46.102(e)). "Intervention" refers to the procedures used to gather data, including but not limited to surveys, interviews, and observations. "Intervention" also includes situations in which researchers manipulate the participants' environment for research purposes, such as randomly assigning participants to an experimental educational program or a standard program. "Interaction" refers to any personal contact or communication between researchers and participants (45 C.F.R. § 46.102(e)(2–3)).

Information is "individually identifiable" if a person's identity can be determined by the investigator or others by looking at the data. Private data are information "about behavior that occurs in a context in which an individual can reasonably expect that no observation or recording is taking place, and information that has been provided for specific purposes by an individual and that the individual can reasonably expect will not be made public" (45 C.F.R. § 46.102(e)(4)). People can reasonably expect that data sources like medical records and educational records will not be made public. People can also reasonably expect that certain types of conversations that take place in private settings—such as a meeting with a bank loan officer or a job interview—will not be observed or recorded.

Scholarly and journalistic activities that focus directly on specific individuals (e.g., biographies), public health surveillance, and the collection of data for criminal justice or federal intelligence investigations are not human subjects research. Other than these, no other specific examples are named in the federal research regulations.

If your IRB determines that your activities are in fact research with human subjects, based on the level of risk, your study may be reviewed by the full board, may be eligible for expedited review (see Questions #78 and #79), or may be determined to be exempt from IRB oversight (see Question #77). It is important to note that even if you think your research meets the criteria for exemption, your protocol must still undergo a form of IRB review.

Depending on your institution, there may be different processes or forms to complete for full board, expedited, or exempt research—as well as for determining whether an activity is human subjects research. Research that poses greater than minimal risk and that must undergo review by the full board is also required to be reviewed periodically—annually or perhaps more frequently—until data collection activities are complete.

More questions? See #78, #79, and #81.

How Do I Know Which IRB—and How Many IRBs—Must Review and Approve My Proposed Research?

If all researchers involved in a proposed research study are at the same institution, then that institution's institutional review board (IRB) will need to review the study. For research conducted in another country by researchers from that country in collaboration with researchers from the United States, the research must be reviewed by the IRB at the U.S. researcher's institution *and* by an IRB or similar body in the country where the research will be conducted.

For U.S.-based, federally funded cooperative research—meaning, research that involves more than one U.S. site—the protocol must be reviewed by a single IRB, starting in 2020 (and in January 2018 for NIH-funded research). Using a single IRB process, only one IRB reviews and approves the research. All other IRBs must provide agreement for this IRB to review the research on their behalf. Exceptions are only possible when multiple reviews are required by law (for example, if research review is also required by another entity, such as with research involving American Indian or Alaskan Native tribes) or if the federal agency sponsoring or conducting the study determines that a review by a single IRB is not appropriate.

Not all IRBs, however, are comfortable with the single IRB approach; therefore, review by multiple IRBs may continue to be the standard for research that is not subject to the federal regulations.

More questions? See #66, #74, and #75.

When Is a Research Study "Exempt" From the Federal Research Regulations, and What Does This Mean?

The federal research regulations outline seven categories of research that are considered "exempt" from following all the regulations—including the requirement for written informed consent—because they pose little risk to participants. However, even research that appears to meet criteria for exemption must be reviewed by someone from the IRB who will decide whether the research is indeed exempt.

In the social and behavioral sciences, research that is typically considered exempt (45 C.F.R. § 46.104) includes

- research involving normal educational practices;
- research involving educational tests, survey or interview procedures, or observation of public behavior that because data are collected anonymously or are not sensitive, poses no risk of harm to "subjects' financial standing, employability, or reputation" and does not put them at risk of "criminal or civil liability";
- research with adults involving brief "benign behavioral interventions";
- research involving the analysis of publicly available data or specimens or data anonymously recorded from private records;
- secondary analysis of data that were or will be collected for nonresearch purposes;
- research on public service or benefit programs; and
- taste and food quality evaluation and consumer acceptance studies.

Investigators whose research falls under one of these categories must typically still submit their protocols and some accompanying materials to their IRBs. IRBs may have specific forms and/or processes for the submission and review of research that will likely be determined to be exempt from federal research regulations. Importantly, researchers conducting studies exempt from federal research regulations must still adhere to basic ethical principles such as treating participants respectfully, providing them with basic information about the study, and storing data in a secure manner.

More questions? See #39, #78, and #80.

What Is Expedited Review?

The federal research regulations outline procedures for the expedited review of research that involves no more than minimal risk but does not otherwise meet exempt criteria (45 C.F.R. § 46.110). In such cases, the full board of an IRB does not typically review the research. Instead, the research proposal is reviewed by the IRB chairperson or by one or more IRB members who are designated by the chairperson. This reviewer can approve the research or ask for modifications. If the reviewer wants to disapprove a research study, then the full board must review it.

Because of the dynamic nature of research, rather than including what types of research are eligible for expedited review in the federal research regulations, a list of such research studies is published on the website of the Office of Human Research Protections (https://www.hhs.gov/ohrp/), the government agency responsible for developing, revising, and enforcing the federal research regulations. The list is periodically reviewed and updated.

More questions? See #13, #77, and #79.

What Is the Difference Between Expedited and Full Board Review?

In expedited review, only one or two designated individuals associated with the IRB reviews the research. In full board review, all members of the IRB review and discuss the research. The level of risk of the proposed research determines the type of review. Research that poses no greater than minimal risk but does not otherwise meet exemption criteria (see Question #77) typically qualifies for expedited review; research that poses more than minimal risk is reviewed by the full board. Depending on the institution, researchers may be specifically asked to justify why their research qualifies for expedited review—that is, why it poses no greater than minimal risk.

Additionally, an expedited review typically takes a shorter period of time, because the designated IRB expedited reviewer can review the research at any time rather than waiting for the full board to meet. And, although research that qualifies for expedited review needs to be reviewed only once, prior to the start of the research, research that poses greater than minimal risk and is initially reviewed by the full IRB must undergo continuing review, usually once a year. Most institutions require the same materials to be submitted whether expedited or full board is required.

More questions? See #13, #78, and #85.

What Materials Will
I Need to Submit to the IRB?

An IRB will generally require submission of a research protocol as well as all recruitment materials, informed consent documents, data collection instruments, and if applicable, intervention materials.

Some institutions have specific application forms or questions that will need to be completed in addition to submission of the research protocol and materials. Many academic institutions have an online submission process.

A thorough, formal research protocol should detail all aspects of the research and study procedures, including

- purpose, aims, and objectives of the research;
- data collection methods and a description of surveys, questionnaires, interview guides, and tools that will be used to collect data;
- a detailed description of the intervention being tested, if applicable;
- duration and location of the study;
- characteristics and number of study participants as well as the process for assigning participants to groups, if applicable;
- justification for enrolling the population you have selected, particularly if you plan to include individuals from vulnerable groups;
- description of recruitment and informed consent procedures, including where recruitment and informed consent will take place and who will be responsible for obtaining consent;
- information about payment or other compensation for participants as well as information about any potential costs that participants may incur;
- assessment of the risks and benefits of participation, and a justification that there is a favorable risk–benefit balance;
- steps that will be taken to minimize risks;
- storage of research materials, including the steps that will be taken to protect participant privacy and the confidentiality of research data;

- preliminary data analysis plans; and
- plans for disseminating research findings.

Research recruitment materials must also be submitted, such as flyers or posters that will be distributed or hung in public places; letters or emails (personalized or mass); other direct mail advertisements; print or Web ads; text for radio spots; and scripts that will be used by individuals making phone calls or in-person requests for participation.

In addition to detailing the informed consent process in the protocol, a copy of any informed consent forms must also be submitted, when appropriate. Most institutions require the use of a specific format as well as specific template language. This information should be found on your IRB's website.

Data collection instruments should be submitted in the format that will be used in the field. However, for some studies, it may be necessary or preferable instead to submit text for instruments that will be later programmed into computer-assisted survey software or web-based programs.

If a research study is testing an intervention, any materials such as presentations, pamphlets, or other educational materials should also be submitted to the IRB. These are necessary to provide context for your research activities and data collection tools.

Most IRBs meet at regular intervals (monthly or bimonthly), and will require investigators with proposals requiring full board review to meet a deadline so that materials can be distributed prior to the meeting. For exempt studies (see Question #77) or those eligible for expedited review (see Questions #78 and #79), these deadlines may not apply.

Throughout the course of a study, you are also responsible for reporting any adverse events and protocol violations (see Questions #96, 97, and 99), and for submitting any planned changes to already approved research (called amendments, see Question #84), as well as any required continuing review reports.

More questions? See #40, #56, and #85.

What Can I Expect During the IRB Review Process?

If your research is federally funded, the IRB reviews your research to ensure that it complies with the federal research regulations and general ethics principles. IRBs usually also apply the federal research regulations to the review of research that is not federally funded. The federal research regulations are broad and do not cover all the issues researchers face in the conduct of research. For example, there is no mention of the use of the Internet to collect data. Therefore, IRBs have discretion to develop their own institutional policies, which they use, in addition to the federal research regulations, when reviewing research. Given the limited guidelines regarding the assessment of risk, research that might be acceptable to one IRB might raise concerns of another. Because of this, the same research study may be approved without modifications by one IRB, but another IRB may require changes.

After your protocol is reviewed by your IRB, you will receive a formal communication in writing (usually an email or a letter) informing you of the final decision or telling you what to do next. If your research is not determined to be exempt, an IRB either approves the study, disapproves the study, or requests modifications to be made prior to final approval. This latter action is most common, and only in very rare cases does an IRB ever completely disapprove a research study. In addition to this prospective review, IRBs have the authority to observe any aspect of a study during implementation, including the informed consent process, although this is uncommon.

Due to the variance in institutional policies, a book like this can never give you all the answers about what to expect during the IRB review process. You'll need to get to know your IRB chair and/or staff members, required submission procedures, and institutional policies as the first step in preparing to submit your research protocol for IRB review.

More questions? See #75, #82, and #83.

Before IRB Approval,
What Can I Do and Not Do?

No recruitment of participants or collection of data may begin until you receive IRB approval or a determination of exemption. You may, however, collect information you need to write your research protocol and accompanying materials and to prepare your IRB submission packet. For example, if you plan to recruit participants from specific sites, you can contact these sites and discuss logistics so you can provide sufficient context in the research protocol. If these sites are outside of your own institution, letters of support and description of the role(s) of site personnel may be required for IRB submission. You may also need to find out from the site basic information about their clients or constituents to determine if the site will yield sufficient numbers of participants. This type of information gathering is allowable as long as the site does not give you any personally identifiable information; the number of clients and basic demographics can be provided rather than lists of client names.

Pretesting or conducting "trial runs" with data collection instruments, such as surveys, with project staff members or other colleagues, is allowed without IRB approval. You can also have scientific experts or community advisory board members review data collection instruments, intervention materials, or recruitment and consent documents prior to IRB approval.

While some IRBs allow pretesting to be done with individuals who are similar to the study population prior to IRB approval as long as data are not stored, some IRBs require the individuals' consent, regardless of what is done with the data. If you want to pretest data collection instruments, and your IRB requires that you seek approval to do this, you can describe how the pretest will be conducted and with whom in your research protocol. You should also indicate whether you will resubmit the final data collection instrument(s) after changes are made from the pretest.

Researchers should complete all required training prior to IRB submission. Any individual who will recruit participants; obtain informed consent from participants; collect, enter, analyze, or have access to data; deliver an intervention; or have any other contact with participants must successfully complete their institution's required human research ethics training in order to be involved in the research.

More questions? See #9, #81, and #84.

What Are Changes That the IRB Can Request, and How Do I Respond?

After initial review of your research protocol, the IRB will send a formal written communication informing you that your research has been approved or disapproved, that modifications are needed, or that it has been determined to be exempt. IRBs often request additional information and/or require changes to make the research consistent with federal research regulations, institutional policy, best practices, and/or ethical principles. Most commonly, IRBs request modifications to consent form language, particularly if language deviates from institutionally required templates, is at too high a reading level, or is poorly written.

In some cases, an IRB may require very specific changes to documents or proposed activities and will be directive regarding the nature and format of these changes. This often occurs when aspects of the proposed research are in direct violation of federal research regulations or institutional policy, for example, if key information is missing from a consent form. When changes are required to achieve regulatory or institutional compliance, IRBs will explain the violation in the letter and outline acceptable options. Generally, however, IRB requests for changes will be nondirective.

Often an IRB will ask for clarification or justification for why you are doing something a particular way. Such a request does not necessarily imply that they want you to do something differently or make a change. Such questions may ask for

- justification of sample size;
- explanation of inclusion–exclusion criteria;
- more details regarding planned recruitment strategies or materials;
- justification of the collection of certain data points that do not seem central to your research question and perhaps pose additional risk;

- more details regarding data collection procedures or data storage methods to ensure appropriate privacy and confidentiality protections; and
- clarification regarding inconsistencies in the protocol or between the protocol and other study documents such as the consent form.

In responding to IRB requests for modifications, you should make the required changes in your protocol and any related documents. You must also detail these changes and provide responses to any questions in a letter responding point by point to the issues outlined in the IRB's letter.

Frequently an IRB's request for modifications will focus on identifying and explaining a particular concern with a proposed study procedure or document, but the IRB will ask the investigator to propose a solution and revise accordingly. In some cases, an IRB may suggest a solution, if for example, a best practice or standard exists; but you may propose an alternative course of action. If the IRB makes a recommendation for a modification that appears binding, and you find the suggestion unsatisfactory, a solid and persuasive ethical justification will be required if you want to pursue another course of action.

Very few institutions have a formal appeals process for investigators to contest decisions made by the IRB. Although you can call your IRB office and talk to a representative, most IRBs prefer communicating with investigators in writing, so they can have a record of decisions made. Face-to-face meetings can also be requested.

More questions? See #6, #80, and #84.

What Should I Do If I Want to Change the Protocol, Consent Form, or Other Documents After They Have Been Approved by an IRB?

Frequently researchers want or need to change some aspect of their research after receiving IRB approval. For example, once you start recruitment, you may realize that something is not working the way you thought it would and people are not enrolling in your study. The need to alter course is a normal part of the research process. However, as a matter of regulations and ethics, most changes need IRB approval before they can be implemented. IRBs want to review the proposed changes to ensure that they do not alter the risks and benefits. This applies to exempt research as well.

Importantly, no change can be implemented until you have submitted what is called an *amendment* to the IRB, AND the IRB approves the amendment. An amendment describes in detail the changes that you want to make to the study or documents and why. You can continue to conduct your research using the previously approved procedures while you wait for the amendment to be approved. However, you cannot implement any of the requested changes, such as a revised consent form or new recruitment approaches, until they are IRB-approved.

Changes that require an amendment include but are not limited to

- the addition of new research personnel;
- changes to the informed consent form or process;
- changes to the inclusion/exclusion criteria;
- changes to your recruitment strategies (including the addition of new recruitment sites) or materials; and
- changes to your data collection instruments (surveys, interview or focus group guides). (Note: Determining what constitutes a

significant change to qualitative research instruments, such as focus group or interview guides, can be tricky. In general, amendments need to be submitted only when new topics are added.)

When submitting an amendment, the IRB usually requests that any revised documents, such as the consent form, be submitted with changes tracked, so that changes can be easily reviewed. If the IRB at your institution stamps documents, then even a minor change to a stamped document—such as a phone number on a consent form—must be submitted as an amendment so that the document can be restamped.

Many amendments can be reviewed through expedited procedures, even if the research was initially reviewed by the full board, when the changes do not affect the risk–benefit balance. Examples include changes to survey instruments or personnel; or changes to an intervention that do not significantly affect content, such as adding or decreasing the number of sessions.

When proposed changes to a protocol are extensive, the IRB may require that enrolled participants be re-consented, meaning that they must review and sign the new consent form in order to continue with the research. For example, re-consent might be needed in a longitudinal study if survey instruments have been changed and will now take much longer to complete or if the later surveys will include sensitive topics that were not previously disclosed in the consent form.

Amendments are also used for research that is conducted in phases—that is, when the specific plans for later phases rely on findings from a previous phase. In submitting a multiphase study to your IRB for the first time, you should (1) provide a comprehensive overview of the first phase of the research, clarifying that you are requesting approval for those activities; and (2) briefly describe what you anticipate the later phases of the research will cover, highlighting that those phases are "to be determined." Be sure to state clearly that amendments will be submitted for later phases and that you will not begin any of the later phases until those amendments have been approved.

More questions? See #6, #82, and #83.

What Should I Do
If My Research Requires
Continuing Review?

If your research poses greater than minimal risk and undergoes review by the full IRB, you will be required to provide updates on your research to your IRB annually, or perhaps more frequently. Continuing review reevaluates the risks of the research and ensures that researchers have adhered to their protocol as approved.

Each IRB has its own forms that researchers are required to submit for the annual review. Typical items that researchers are asked to report are

- an update on study status—for example, that enrollment and data collection are still ongoing or that enrollment is closed and data are being analyzed;
- the number of participants who have enrolled;
- the number of participants who have dropped out or have been withdrawn by the researcher;
- information on participant safety, such as a summary of adverse events reported and not yet reported to the IRB;
- any new findings related to your research that may affect risks to participants and, therefore, changes to the informed consent form; and
- any publications or presentations that report findings.

Researchers are also required to resubmit key documents such as the protocol and consent forms.

The time period for your continuing review (usually one year) will be listed on your initial approval letter. Most IRBs will send you a reminder when the deadline for continuing review is approaching. If you miss the deadline for submitting materials for IRB continuing review, your IRB may require that all research activities be temporarily stopped until they rereview and approve the research.

For those studies that require continuing review, reporting should continue until all data have been collected and the researchers no longer have contact with study participants. Check with your IRB regarding the process for indicating when data collection has ended, as well as for closing a research study.

More questions? See #6, #79, and #89.

I Am Collecting Data for a Class Project. Do I Need IRB Approval?

The answer to this question depends on the specific rules at your institution. Assuming that your class project is not funded by a federal research grant, some IRBs require that all student research projects be submitted for IRB review while others do not, particularly if the data will be used only for a class paper or presentation. If you must submit your proposed research to your IRB, the review may be done by the institution's IRB chairperson, a designated IRB member, or another review group or individual. Or, an institution may have a separate process for reviewing classroom-based projects.

Importantly, requiring IRB or similar review of student research promotes the ethical treatment of those participating, even if they are not *technically* human research subjects. Such review ensures that student researchers are using appropriate privacy and confidentiality protections, because student research can still have negative consequences for participants if their identities become known or if there is a breach in confidentiality of their data. Such review can have practical or scientific implications as well. Requiring IRB or similar review gives students valuable experience with submitting research for ethics review.

If you are collecting data for a class project, your instructor should be familiar with the institutional rules about classroom data collection and IRB review. If you are collecting data for a class project and your instructor has not yet introduced the topic of research ethics or IRBs, ask him or her about your institution's policies.

More questions? See #10, #74, and #75.

I Am Conducting an Evaluation of a Program. Do I Need IRB Approval?

Evaluations of social programs that are federally funded are listed as an exempt category in the federal research regulations. However, evaluation of non–federally funded programs may require IRB review. Some program evaluation activities that involve gathering information from or about humans do not necessarily aim to produce generalizable knowledge and, therefore, may not require IRB review.

Although the data collection activities used in program evaluation and research are similar, such as surveys or focus groups, program evaluation and research have different goals and purposes. Understanding these differences is helpful in determining whether IRB approval is needed for program evaluation. Program evaluation aims to determine how well a specific program works in a particular setting; research aims to generate new knowledge that can be extrapolated to an entire population. Program evaluation aims to inform future decisions about the program, such as whether and how it will continue; research aims to establish causation. Many projects involve elements of both program evaluation and research.

To determine whether an evaluation of a program requires IRB review, consider how the results will be used. If the evaluators plan to use the results to improve their program for the participants at their organization—for example, by identifying and removing those sessions previous participants found least useful—the activities are likely program evaluation and do not need IRB approval. If the evaluators want to use the results to suggest that this program is responsible for participants' changing a behavior and to recommend that the program be used with other populations, then the activities are likely research and need IRB approval.

Here is an example to illustrate the difference between research and program evaluation. A researcher is conducting an evaluation to determine whether a new weight loss program is effective in adults over 65 years old. Interested participants at a local senior center are randomized into two groups—a group that participates in the new weight loss program and a group that participates in the old weight loss program. At the end of the program, the researcher compares the amount of weight loss between the two groups. Participants in the new weight loss program lost more weight. The researcher then publishes the findings in a journal publication and suggests that senior centers nationwide implement the new program. These activities are considered human subjects research.

Now consider that instead of evaluating whether a new program is more effective than an old program, all participants receive the same weight loss program and the goal is to determine how to make the program better for people at the senior center who will participate in it next year. The data-gathering activities focus primarily on participant satisfaction (e.g., questions about the time, location, instructor, activities). This will likely be considered program evaluation, not human subjects research, and will therefore not require IRB review.

Based on the above examples, you can see that the primary difference between program evaluation and research is related to intention. However, even if your original intent is program improvement, you may realize midcourse that you want to tell others about your findings so they can use them to improve their own programs (that is, generalize findings to populations beyond those currently involved in the program) or to build on your results. Many journals require proof of IRB approval (or a determination that data collection activities are either exempt or otherwise not subject to IRB review). So, what do you do if you conducted a program evaluation without IRB approval and you now want to publish the results? You can seek an IRB determination of exemption before publishing the data, if certain criteria are met.

Importantly, program evaluation is not without ethical concerns, regardless of whether it is considered research or not. Program evaluation activities may still pose risks to participants; for example, if private, personal information is collected by the evaluators, there is a risk of a breach of confidentiality and potential harm from a breach. Even if the activity is not considered research, evaluators should always explain the purposes of data collection activities to participants and inform them that participation in program evaluation activities is voluntary.

More questions? See #51, #75, and #77.

PART 9

UNDERSTANDING ETHICAL RESPONSIBILITIES OF DATA USE

What Confidentiality Procedures Should I Put in Place After All Data Have Been Collected?

Once all data have been collected, you should continue to follow procedures that will reduce the likelihood of a breach of confidentiality. According to the federal research regulations, however, the need for confidentiality procedures depends on whether identifiers are linked to the data in any way.

If participants' identities can be determined by viewing the research files, you must keep all confidentiality procedures in place until the data are de-identified or the data are destroyed according to the study protocol approved by your institutional review board. This includes situations when you have a master code list linking participants' contact information with their participant identification codes or when the data include personal identifiers or contextual information that could identify the participants.

If data are anonymous or have been de-identified, you are not required to protect data in the same way as identifiable data. However, it still is a good practice to maintain the same or similar confidentiality protections.

You should consider the necessity of keeping participant identifiers, because it increases the likelihood that participants can or will be identified if there is a breach in confidentiality. Ask yourself which identifiable information should be retained and which is no longer necessary to be linked with the data. This is particularly relevant after the data are analyzed and manuscripts describing the data are published. Researchers should keep only those identifiers that are necessary for completing any remaining research activities.

More questions? See #19, #20, and #23.

How Long Must
I Keep My Research Records?

The federal research regulations do not specify how long research records (such as transcripts from participant interviews) should be stored. You should consult the retention requirements specified by your funder and institution. For example, both the National Institutes of Health (NIH) and the National Science Foundation (NSF) generally require that the research records be kept for 3 years. Research data that involve medical records are also subject to Health Insurance Portability and Accountability Act (HIPAA) regulations that require research files to be stored for 6 years. Retention requirements apply to both electronic and paper files. In the social and behavioral sciences, the following research records are typically stored:

- study protocol
- standard operating procedures
- signed consent forms
- field notes
- transcripts
- completed questionnaires
- electronic databases
- analysis notes
- IRB communications

When funder and institutional policies conflict, you should follow the longer storage requirement. For example, if your research study is funded by an agency that requires research records to be stored for 3 years and your institutional policy states that files should be stored for 5 years, you should retain the files for 5 years.

Funder and institutional policies also describe when the storage time period is to begin. For some policies, the storage retention period starts when the study team no longer has any contact with study participants, that is, after all data have been collected. For others, retention starts when the analysis of identifiable study data is completed. Both NIH and NSF specify that the retention period starts after they receive the last study report from the researcher.

While following confidentiality procedures and approval from your institutional review board, you may want to keep indefinitely research files that support and demonstrate how your study's findings were generated, in case the findings are ever questioned by other researchers. You may also want to retain documentation that demonstrates that all ethical requirements were followed (such as that informed consent was obtained from each participant).

More questions? See #80, #88, and #90.

When Can I Destroy
My Research Files?

After research files have been stored for the maximum time period, you can destroy them. However, some researchers prefer to maintain at least some of their files past the maximum retention time period. You must balance the necessity of retaining research records (after the specified time period) with the ongoing risk to participants from not destroying the files. If identifiers are linked with the data, the risk of a breach of confidentiality remains for as long as those data are stored. Therefore, if retaining research files after the maximum retention time period is unnecessary, then they should likely be destroyed; if not destroyed, they should likely be de-identified. If identifiers are not linked with the study data, the need to destroy research files after the maximum retention time period becomes far less urgent and likely not necessary at all.

Research storage space is a consideration when deciding when to destroy files after the maximum retention time period; storage space for paper documents is often difficult to find and may be costly. However, handwritten research notes and other hard copy documents can be electronically scanned, as electronic files are much easier to store over time.

Signed consent forms can also be destroyed at the end of the maximum retention time period. Electronic records, such as databases and typed transcripts, can also be destroyed at this time if all of the study's manuscripts have been published, and you believe the study's results will not be questioned to the extent that the original files must be accessed and data re-verified. Some researchers prefer to maintain electronic data indefinitely, out of anticipation that the data could be used in secondary analysis in the future, for example. If data are truly de-identified, there is no ethical reason to delete research files.

Audio files from interviews are sometimes destroyed *before* the maximum retention time period, with the permission of the institutional review board (IRB). In fact, most IRBs require that audio files be destroyed at some point before data are placed into long-term storage. This is because audio files contain participants' voices, which can be uniquely identifiable if accessed. Additionally, participants might not want the audio recording from their interview (or any other of their research files for that matter) to be retained endlessly. Some researchers wait to destroy audio files until the typed transcripts have been verified to ensure that the typed transcript corresponds with what was said in the audio file. Other researchers prefer to wait to destroy audio files until the study manuscripts are published, in case they need to review the original source of the data during the peer review of the manuscript.

Depending on the type of study, you can destroy handwritten field notes earlier than other research records, with permission of your IRB. In these situations, handwritten documents are typed or scanned, and then those files are stored electronically for the maximum retention time period. After these documents become electronic, the original handwritten versions can be destroyed. However, if handwritten field notes are your only source of data and you prefer not to—or are unable to—scan the documents, they should be stored for at least the maximum retention time period. All paper research files should be shredded, as opposed to simply thrown away; shredded documents can be recycled.

You should develop instructions for study staff members to follow that specify how long different types of research files will be retained and destroyed, and how each type of file will be destroyed. Additionally, you should consider maintaining a log that documents specifically what was destroyed, and how and when it was destroyed.

While different researchers will have different preferences for when to destroy research files, you should describe your plans to retain and destroy research files in your study protocol, so your IRB can review and approve your plans. These procedures should also be described in the study's consent forms, so prospective participants can consider this information when they make an informed decision about study participation.

More questions? See #19, #23, and #89.

Do I Have an Ethical Obligation to Publish My Research Findings?

Regardless of whether you are an academic researcher or a researcher from another kind of institution, it is important to recognize the research process does not end once your data are collected and analyzed. Disseminating your study findings—and considering what future research is now needed—is part of the overall research process. Research in the social and behavioral sciences can advance only if researchers inform others in their field of their research findings. Publication allows other researchers to provide constructive criticism of the published research findings and build on them, therefore not wasting time and resources duplicating efforts.

Publishing research findings also honors the time and resources spent conducting the research. Participants took time out of their daily lives to share their experiences with you. Funding agencies gave you funding to conduct the research. Disseminating study findings allows participants' voices be heard.

Additionally, if you are an academic researcher, publishing research findings is an expected, fundamental activity. Not only is it important for you to share your findings with the scientific community for the sake of contributing to science, but your career advancement in academia is typically dependent on peer-reviewed publications.

More questions? See #1, #2, and #95.

Can I Publish My Findings If I Did Not Get IRB Approval or Obtain Informed Consent From Participants?

When researchers submit their manuscripts to academic journals for peer review, they are typically required to state as part of the submission process that they followed general ethical principles when conducting the research. At a minimum, journals want confirmation that the research was reviewed by an institutional review board (IRB) and that participants gave their informed consent to participate (or that appropriate waivers were obtained), or that the research was determined to be exempt from the federal research regulations. Within the manuscript text, researchers must describe that they received ethics approval or an exempt determination (and often give the name of reviewing IRB) and, if applicable, describe how informed consent was obtained from participants. It will likely be difficult for you to publish your research findings in reputable journals if the research was not reviewed by an IRB.

More questions? See #6, #37, and #77.

What Do I Need to Do to Ensure That I Protect Participants' Identities When Sharing Datasets With Others and That Participants Are Informed of This Possibility?

S ome funding agencies request or require that data collected from the research they fund be made accessible to other researchers and the public. For example, during the Obama administration, the federal government stated that all data from federally funded research that have been published in peer-reviewed, scholarly journals be made available for use by the public, industry, and the scientific community, to the extent allowed by law. As a result, federal agencies, such as the National Institutes of Health (NIH) and the United States Agency for International Development (USAID), have issued guidance to facilitate the process. Researchers who expect to share their datasets publicly should be familiar with their funders' guidance describing the kinds of data that should be included, such as survey data, and how they should be accessible, such as through the funder's repository.

When preparing data to be shared, you must consider how to protect the personal identifiers that are linked with those data. For data that are to be widely shared—that is, with unrestricted access to anyone who wants to use the data—you typically must remove all personal identifiers from the data before the dataset can be uploaded to any data repository. Additionally, you may need to remove any possibility of re-identifying participants using other means, such as destroying a master list linking participants' contact information with their participant identification code. For data that are to be shared directly with other researchers, and not be made publicly available, you (as the original researcher) must still remove any personally identifiable information from the data; however, you can likely retain means for re-identification (such as code lists).

The above guidelines generally refer to quantitative data. You should review your funders' guidance on how to share qualitative data; they may suggest that it not be shared at all. Given the nature of qualitative research, it may be too difficult protect participants' identities when sharing transcripts; and audio files should never be shared.

Participants should be informed during the informed consent process that their data may be shared publicly and/or with other researchers, once de-identified. A statement such as the following could be included in the consent form: "The information you provide will be shared publicly. However, before any information is shared, we will remove the personal information that can identify you." If you will keep the master code list, this should also be described.

You should also include a statement in the protocol submitted to your institutional review board that you plan to share the data broadly and describe how you plan to share them, according to the funder's requirement.

More questions? See #19, #24, and #95.

Can I Show Participants Their Transcripts or the Transcripts of Other Participants?

Ethically, it is permissible to share with participants their own transcript from a one-on-one interview, preferably as a PDF (Portable Document Format) so that the content cannot be easily altered. Many researchers believe that participants "own" their data and therefore have the right to view them. In no circumstances are you allowed to share with participants the interview transcripts from other participants. Focus group transcripts are typically not shared when requested by participants because of the potential to identify other participants in the group. If a participant requests to see the transcript from his or her own focus group, you can offer to provide the participant with a summary of the aggregated data.

Before sharing interview transcripts with participants, you should consider whether any possible harm could result. For example, participants could relive a negative experience they described during the interview, when reviewing the transcript. In situations where harm is possible, you can elect to not share the transcript. Or, you can meet in person with the participant and have systems in place for referring her or him to a professional if she or he experiences any emotional harm while reading the transcript. Consult your institutional review board if you are unsure whether a transcript should be shared.

Some researchers conduct a process called "member checking," where they meet again with participants to discuss and verify the data collected via interviews or focus group discussions. There are many methodology considerations for how and when to share data during member checking, but it is ethically acceptable to share with participants their own interview transcript for the purposes of further discussion and verification. For member checking findings from focus group discussions, however, data are typically presented to participants in aggregate, after any identifiable information has been removed.

When sharing interview transcripts, you should request that participants keep the transcript confidential and not share it with others.

However, you cannot control what participants do with their own transcripts. For this reason, you may choose to share transcripts after the data have been de-identified and the primary manuscript has been published. Additionally, you should document and date these requests. If the participant shares the transcript publicly and a negative consequence results, such documentation can help you avoid being accused of a breach in confidentiality.

If you share transcripts, there is a possibility that participants will request that their information be modified in some way. Upon reading the content of a transcript, participants may feel differently about the topic or embarrassed at what they previously said, for example, and request that their transcript be changed. You should establish a policy on how to address requests to change original data.

More questions? See #17, #24, and #95.

Should I Share the Results of My Research With Study Participants?

You should consider sharing your research results with the participants who took part in your study. Participants took time from their busy, daily lives to share their experiences, thoughts, opinions, or recommendations with you. Providing a summary of the results to participants shows that you value and respect their time and input. Additionally, many participants are likely curious about the results of your research. Usually a short one- or two-page summary, written in language understandable to the study participants, will suffice.

Participants also have the right to elect *not* to be informed of the research findings. A good practice is to ask participants their preferences at the time the data are collected. Participants who wish to receive the research results can provide their preferred means of contact for receiving the results, and you can provide the results when they are available. You must take care to ensure that this contact information is stored separately from the participants' data.

You should also consider the research topic prior to deciding whether research results will be shared with participants. If you believe that social or emotional harms may result from the sharing of study results—for example, findings suggest that participants have poor coping skills or unrealistic beliefs—partner with a local community group that is familiar with the study population to determine how best to describe the results to the study population.

When you share research findings with participants, you must ensure that data are provided in aggregate form. Importantly, the information provided cannot be personally identifiable. In particular, you should pay close attention to ensuring that all quotes provided are not identifiable to those other than the participant who provided the quote.

The timing of providing research results to study participants will vary depending on the wishes of the researcher and other factors, such as journal submissions and conference embargos (that is—often conferences do not allow researchers to disclose their research results to others until after the conference presentation on the study's results). Some researchers believe, however, that participants should be the first to know the study results. In these situations, researchers facilitate the release of the research results to participants immediately prior to a conference presentation or journal publication (with approval) or at the same time. Sharing study findings with participants does not constitute prior publication of research results, and therefore does not negatively impact the submission of the research findings for publication.

Ideally you should describe your plans for sharing research results with study participants in your study protocol.

More questions? See #64, #91, and #94.

PART 10

HANDLING ETHICAL ISSUES THAT ARISE DURING RESEARCH IMPLEMENTATION

What Should I Do If I—or a Study Staff Member or Participant—Do Something That Was Not in the Approved Protocol?

Research protocols describe all the activities to be conducted as part of the research. Before any research-related activities are implemented with study participants, the protocol must be reviewed by an institutional review board (IRB). Once reviewed, researchers and other study staff members must follow the approved protocol. Any changes to the approved study activities that are implemented by you or study staff members during the conduct of the research—whether accidental or intentional—are considered to be violations that must be documented and possibly reported. For example, you or a staff member may accidentally enroll an individual who does not meet the eligibility criteria or forget to obtain a signature on an informed consent form prior to administering a survey.

All IRBs set forth guidance on how researchers should handle such situations if they arise in the conduct of a research study. However, IRBs use different terms to describe and categorize unplanned or unanticipated changes, such as major and minor protocol violations, protocol deviations, and incidents.

IRBs typically want any violation, deviation, or incident that poses an unanticipated risk to study participants reported to them within a short period of time. IRBs also typically want promptly reported the failure to obtain informed consent from an individual or any situation that jeopardizes the integrity of study data, such as if study staff members falsify data on a study questionnaire. IRBs often have report templates for researchers to document specific details of the unplanned event.

Minor violations, deviations, and incidents, such as the failure to administer a questionnaire to a study participant, often can be reported to IRBs at the time of annual renewal or documented in the study's files, according to the IRB's policy.

Although not common in social and behavioral sciences research, you are allowed to implement changes to your approved study protocol if the change is necessary to ensure participant safety. In these situations, you implement the change but then subsequently report the incident to your IRB within a relatively short period of time, according to your IRB's policy.

When any violation occurs, regardless of its severity, you should develop a corrective action plan to prevent future similar incidents. Modifications to the study protocol may be necessary. Any changes made to the study protocol must be submitted as an amendment and approved by your IRB before they can be implemented with study participants. In some situations, additional training may be needed for study staff members to ensure that study procedures are fully understood.

The information described above pertains to deviations or changes involving researchers and study staff members. At times participants do not follow study procedures as described in the approved protocol. For example, participants do not complete their at-home diaries. These situations are typically not considered a protocol violation or deviation and do not need to be reported to IRBs.

More questions? See #6, #84, and #99.

What Should I Do If Someone Is Physically, Emotionally, or Socially Harmed From Taking Part in My Research?

Participant safety is the utmost priority of any researcher. If participants are physically or emotionally harmed from participating in your research, you are responsible for helping them get the services they need.

In research where risks of physical or emotional harm are possible, you should establish referral systems with appropriate health care providers or organizations to provide services to participants if they experience harm. The services to be provided are described in the protocol; if such services are not established, they may be requested by your institutional review board (IRB). You should also establish procedures for monitoring participants for harm and for following up with participants (with their permission) to ensure that they have received the needed care.

Your IRB must also be notified when participants experience harm. Details such as when the harm occurred, whether the harm was anticipated, what services were provided to the participant, and what the study team is doing to limit reoccurrence of this harm (if unanticipated) should be reported to your IRB.

More questions? See #11, #12, and #17.

What Should I Do If a Participant Says He Wants to Harm Himself or Someone Else?

Although infrequent, a participant may describe intentions to harm him- or herself or others—or report that he or she is currently causing harm to someone else, such as child neglect or domestic violence. You should check your state laws and your institutional review board's (IRB) policy for handling these situations. Typically, researchers are obligated to contact the appropriate authorities when a participant discloses such information. Additionally, if you anticipate that this could occur during your research, you should describe in the informed consent form that you must contact the appropriate authorities if a participant describes harming him- or herself or others. Participants must be informed of situations in which the confidentiality of their data will not be maintained by you because of state laws or IRB policy.

More questions? See #23, #24, and #31.

What Should I Do If I Lose My Field Notes or Other Hard Copies of Data?

You must take great care to ensure that any study data that exist on paper, including copies of surveys and field notes, are kept secure. If participant data are misplaced and cannot be found, you must contact your institutional review board (IRB), even if the data are anonymous.

Your IRB will likely want to know what kind of data were lost, how many participants are affected, what personal identifiers were included, and approximately where the data were lost. You will need to consider and explain to your IRB whether participants could possibly be identified if someone else were to access the missing data, particularly if personal identifiers are linked in any way with the data. If it is possible that participants' identities can be discovered, you will need to explain whether there a potential for harm to them if others see their data, such as responses to sensitive survey questions.

Your IRB will advise on the necessity of informing participants about the missing data, and may request that additional procedures be established to prevent the future loss of study data. Based on the severity of the breach and any resultant harm, your IRB may decide to stop the study.

Although beyond the scope of this book, researchers also must decide how the missing data will impact the integrity of their study, assuming it continues. For example, researchers must decide whether they will need to recollect lost data from the same study participants or whether new study participants should be enrolled. Either action would require submission of an IRB amendment.

More questions? See #20, #23, and #96.

What Should I Do If a Participant Says a Person's Name or the Name of an Organization During an Interview or Focus Group Discussion?

To limit the collection of identifiable information, researchers typically ask participants at the start of an interview or focus group to refrain from using personal and organizational names (unless organizational names are directly related to the study objective). Instead, participants are asked to broadly describe the relationship of that person to them (e.g., my friend) or the type of organization (e.g., my church). However, there is no guarantee that participants will follow this requested guidance.

When personal and organizational names are mentioned in interviews and focus groups, you should omit them from your field notes and instead indicate the type of relationship or organization that is described. During transcription, personal and organizational names should also be omitted and replaced with a description of the person or organization. For example, the transcriptionist should type [name of friend] or [name of organization] in the space where the participant said the actual name during the interview or focus group: "I got a lot of help from [my friend] during this time." Using this approach, the researcher is aware of the relationship during analysis, but the personal name or organization is omitted, thus making the person or organization less identifiable.

More questions? See #19, #22, and #23.

References
and Resources

Part 1: Understanding Ethics in Research With Human Participants

Ethics Resources From Major Professional Associations

American Anthropological Association, Ethics resources. Retrieved from http://www.americananthro.org/ParticipateAndAdvocate/Content.aspx?ItemNumber=1895

American Association for Public Opinion Research, Standards and Ethics, *AAPOR Code of Ethics*. Retrieved from http://www.aapor.org/Standards-Ethics/AAPOR-Code-of-Ethics.aspx

American Educational Research Association, Professional and Research Ethics, *AERA Code of Ethics*. Retrieved from http://www.aera.net/About-AERA/AERA-Rules-Policies/Professional-Ethics

American Evaluation Association, *Guiding principles for evaluators*. Retrieved from http://www.eval.org/p/cm/ld/fid=51

American Psychological Association, *Ethical principles of psychologists and Code of Conduct*. Retrieved from http://www.apa.org/ethics/code/index.aspx

American Public Health Association, Ethics, Resources. Retrieved from https://www.apha.org/apha-communities/member-sections/ethics/resources

American Sociological Association, *Code of Ethics*. Retrieved from http://www.asanet.org/membership/code-ethics

National Association of Social Workers, *Code of Ethics*. Retrieved from https://www.socialworkers.org/pubs/code/default.asp

Federal Research Regulations and Guidance

Office of Human Research Protections, U.S. Department of Health and Human Services. Retrieved from https://www.hhs.gov/ohrp/

Secretary's Advisory Committee on Human Research Protections. Retrieved from https://www.hhs.gov/ohrp/sachrp-committee/index.html

Foundational Works on Research Ethics

Council for International Organizations of Medical Sciences (CIOMS) & World Health Organization (WHO). (2016). *International ethical guidelines for health-related research involving humans*. Retrieved from https://cioms.ch/shop/product/international-ethical-guidelines-for-health-related-research-involving-humans/

Jonas, H. (1969). Philosophical reflections on experimenting with human subjects. *Daedalus, 98*, 219–247.

National Commission for the Protection of Human Subjects of Biomedical and Behavioral Research. (1979). *The Belmont Report: Ethical principles and guidelines for the protection of human subjects of research*. Retrieved from https://www.hhs.gov/ohrp/regulations-and-policy/belmont-report/index.html

The Nuremberg Code. (1947). *Trials of war criminals before the Nuremberg military tribunals under Control Council Law*. No. 10, Vol. 2. (pp. 181–182). Washington, DC: Government Printing Office. Retrieved from https://history.nih.gov/research/downloads/nuremberg.pdf

World Medical Association. (2013). *Declaration of Helsinki: Ethical principles for medical research involving human subjects*. Retrieved from https://www.wma.net/policies-post/wma-declaration-of-helsinki-ethical-principles-for-medical-research-involving-human-subjects/ (Original work published 1964)

Ethically Controversial Research

Primary Sources

Goffman, A. (2014). *On the run: Fugitive life in an American city*. Illinois: University of Chicago Press.

Good, K. (1991). *Into the heart: One man's pursuit of love and knowledge among the Yanomami*. New York, NY: Simon & Schuster.

Humphreys, L. (1975). *Tearoom trade: Impersonal sex in public places*. New York, NY: Aldine.

Milgram, S. (2009). *Obedience to authority: An experimental view*. New York, NY: Harper Perennial Modern Classics. (Original work published 1974)

Venkatesh, S. (2008). *Gang leader for a day: A rogue sociologist takes to the streets*. New York, NY: Penguin.

Wolcott, H. F. (2002). *The sneaky kid and its aftermath: Ethics and intimacy in fieldwork*. Walnut Creek, CA: Altamira Press.

Zimbardo, P. *The Stanford prison experiment*. Retrieved from the website http://www.prisonexp.org/

Critiques

Calvey, D. (2017). *Covert research: The art, politics, and ethics of undercover fieldwork*. Thousand Oaks, CA: Sage.

Jones, J. H. (1993). *Bad blood: The Tuskegee syphilis experiment*. New York, NY: Free Press.

Korn, J. H. (1997). *Illusions of reality: A history of deception in social psychology.* Albany, NY: SUNY Press.

Perry, G. (2013). *Behind the shock machine: The untold story of the notorious Milgram psychology experiments.* New York, NY: New Press.

Part 2: Assessing Research Risks and Benefits

Appelbaum, P. S., Roth, L. H., & Lidz, C. (1982). The therapeutic misconception: Informed consent in psychiatric research. *International Journal of Law and Psychiatry, 5*(3-4), 319–329.

Campbell, R. T. (2003, April). Risk and harm issues in social science research. Position paper prepared for Human Subjects Policy Conference, University of Illinois at Urbana-Champaign. Retrieved from http://xtf.grainger.illinois .edu:8080/xtfEthics/data/gunsalus/risk_and_harm_v2rc/risk_and_harm_v2rc .pdf

Citro, C. F., Ilgen, D. R., & Marrett, C. B. (Eds.). (2003). *Protecting participants and facilitating social and behavioral sciences research.* Washington, DC: The National Academies Press; 2003. (National Research Council; Panel on Institutional Review Boards, Surveys, and Social Science Research; and Committee on National Statistics and Board on Behavioral, Cognitive, and Sensory Sciences).

National Bioethics Advisory Commission. (2001). Assessing risks and potential benefits and evaluating vulnerability. In *Report on ethical and policy issues in research involving human participants* (Vol. 1, Ch. 4). Bethesda, MD: Author.

Prentice, E. D., & Gordon, B. G. (2001). Institutional Review Board assessment of risks and benefits associated with research. In *Report on ethical and policy issues in research involving human participants* (Vol. 2, Commissioned papers and staff analysis). Bethesda, MD: National Bioethics Advisory Commission.

Weijer, C. (2001). The ethical analysis of risks and potential benefits in human subjects research: History, theory, and implications for U.S. regulation. In *Report on ethical and policy issues in research involving human participants* (Vol. 2, Commissioned papers and staff analysis). Bethesda, MD: National Bioethics Advisory Commission.

Part 3: Protecting Privacy and Confidentiality

Ember, C., & Hanisch, R. (2013). *Sustaining domain repositories for digital data: A white paper.* Retrieved from http://datacommunity.icpsr.umich.edu/sites/ default/files/WhitePaper_ICPSR_SDRDD_121113.pdf

Federal Education Rights and Privacy Act (FERPA), 20 U.S.C. § 1232g. See http:// familypolicy.ed.gov/faq-page/ferpa-parents-and-eligible-students#t52n50

Folkman, S. (2000). Privacy and confidentiality. In B. D. Sales & S. Folkman (Eds.), *Ethics in research with human subjects* (pp. 13–26). Washington, DC: American Psychological Association.

Health Insurance Portability and Accountability Act (HIPPA), 42 U.S.C. § 1320.

National Institutes of Health. (2017). *Certificates of Confidentiality (CoC) Kiosk.* Retrieved from https://humansubjects.nih.gov/coc/index

U.S. Department of Education. (2017). *Protecting student privacy: What is the Family Educational Rights and Privacy Act (FERPA)?* Retrieved from https://studentprivacy.ed.gov/

U.S. Department of Health and Human Services, Office for Civil Rights. (2015a). *Guidance regarding methods for de-identification of protected health information in accordance with the Health Insurance Portability and Accountability Act (HIPAA) Privacy Rule.* Retrieved from https://www.hhs.gov/hipaa/for-professionals/privacy/special-topics/de-identification/index.html

U.S. Department of Health and Human Services, Office for Civil Rights. (2015b). *Health Insurance Portability and Accountability Act (HIPAA) Privacy Rule.* Retrieved from https://www.hhs.gov/hipaa/for-professionals/privacy/index.html

Part 4: Protecting Vulnerable Populations

Alderson, P., & Morrow, V. (2011). *The ethics of research with children and young people: A practical handbook.* Thousand Oaks, CA: Sage.

DuBois, J. M., Beskow, L., Campbell, J., Dugosh, K., Festinger, D., Hartz, S., . . . Lidz, C. (2012). Restoring balance: A consensus paper on the protection of vulnerable research participants. *American Journal of Public Health, 102,* 2220–2225.

Fisher, C. B. (1999). Relational ethics and research with vulnerable populations. In National Bioethics Advisory Commission [NBAC], *Reports on research involving persons with mental disorders that may affect decision-making capacity* (Vol. 2, pp. 29–49). Rockville, MD: Commissioned Papers by the NBAC. Retrieved from http://hdl.handle.net/10822/1038248

Fisher, C. B., & Goodman, S. J. (2009). Goodness-of-fit ethics for non-intervention research involving dangerous and illegal behaviors. In Buchanan, D., Fisher, C. B., & Gable, L. (Eds.), *Research with high-risk populations: Balancing science, ethics, and law* (pp. 25–46). Washington, DC: American Psychological Association.

Fisher, C. B., & Ragsdale, K. (2005). Goodness-of-fit ethics for multicultural research. In Trimble, J., & Fisher, C. B. (Eds.), *The handbook of ethical research with ethnocultural populations and communities* (pp. 3–26). Thousand Oaks, CA: Sage.

Kipnis, K. (2001). Vulnerability in research subjects: A bioethical taxonomy. In National Bioethics Advisory Commission [NBAC], *Ethical and policy issues in research involving human participants* (Vol. II, G1–G13). Rockville, MD: Commissioned Papers by the NBAC. Retrieved from http://hdl.handle.net/10822/941754

National Commission for the Protection of Human Subjects of Biomedical and Behavioral Research. (1979). *The Belmont Report: Ethical principles and guidelines for the protection of human subjects of research*. Retrieved from https://www.hhs.gov/ohrp/regulations-and-policy/belmont-report/index.html

Newman, E., Risch, E., & Kassam-Adams, N. (2006). Ethical issues in trauma-related research: A review. *Journal of Empirical Research on Human Research Ethics, 1*(3), 29–46.

Part 5: Obtaining Informed Consent

Appelbaum, P. S., & Grisso, T. (2001). *The MacArthur Competence Assessment Tool for Clinical Research (MacCAT-CR)*. Sarasota, FL: Professional Resource Press.

Beauchamp, T. (2011). Informed consent: Its history, meaning, and present challenges. *Cambridge Quarterly of Healthcare Ethics, 20,* 515–523.

Birbili, M. (2000). Translating from one language to another. *Social Research Update, 31.* University of Surrey. Retrieved from http://sru.soc.surrey.ac.uk/SRU31.html

Denzin, E. M., Santibanez, M. E. B., Moore, H., Foley, A., Gersten, I. D., Gurgol, C., . . . Murphy, E. A. (2012). Easy-to-read informed consent forms for hematopoietic cell transplantation clinical trials. *Biology of Blood and Marrow Transplantation, 18,* 183–189.

Faden, R. R., Beauchamp, T. L. , & King, N. M. (1986). *A history and theory of informed consent*. New York, NY: Oxford University Press.

Hallinan, Z. P., Forrest A., Uhlenbrauck, G., Young, S., & McKinney, R., Jr. (2016). Barriers to change in the informed consent process: A systematic literature review. *IRB: Ethics & Human Research, 38*(3), 1–10.

Institute of Medicine, Board on Population Health and Public Health Practice, Roundtable on Health Literacy. (2015). *Informed consent and health literacy: Workshop summary*. Retrieved from http://nationalacademies.org/hmd/reports/2015/informed-consent-health-literacy.aspx

National Bioethics Advisory Committee (NBAC). (2001). Voluntary informed consent. In *Ethical and policy issues in international research: Clinical trials in developing countries* (Vol. 1., pp. 35–53). Bethesda, MD: Author. Retrieved from https://repository.library.georgetown.edu/bitstream/handle/10822/559362/nbac_international.pdf?sequence=1&isAllowed=y

National Commission for the Protection of Human Subjects of Biomedical and Behavioral Research. (1979). *The Belmont Report: Ethical principles and guidelines for the protection of human subjects of research*. Retrieved from https://www.hhs.gov/ohrp/regulations-and-policy/belmont-report/index.html

Part 6: Designing Ethical Research

American Evaluation Association. (2011). *Statement on cultural competence in evaluation*. Retrieved from http://www.eval.org/ccstatement

American Psychological Association, *Ethical principles of psychologists and Code of Conduct*. Retrieved from http://www.apa.org/ethics/code/index.aspx

Anderson, E. E., Solomon, S., Heitman, E., DuBois, J. M., Fisher, C. B., Kost, R. G., & Ross, L. F. (2012). Research ethics education for community-engaged research: A review and research agenda. *Journal of Empirical Research on Human Research Ethics, 7*(2), 3–19.

Grady, C. (2005). Payment of clinical research subjects. *Journal of Clinical Investigation, 115,* 1681–1687.

Lavery, J. V., Grady, C., Wahl, E. R., & Emanuel, E. J. (2007). *Ethical issues in international biomedical research: A casebook.* New York, NY: Oxford University Press.

Milgram, S. (2009). *Obedience to authority: An experimental view.* New York, NY: Harper Perennial Modern Classics. (Original work published 1974)

Santos, L. (2008, Winter). Genetic research in Native communities. *Progressive Community Health Partnerships: Research, Education, and Action, 2,* 321–327. Retrieved from https://www.ncbi.nim.nih.gov/pmc/articles/PMC2862689/

Scott-Jones, D. (2000). Recruitment of research participants. In B. D. Sales & S. Folkman (Eds.), *Ethics in research with human subjects* (pp. 27–34). Washington, DC: American Psychological Association.

Sieber, J. E., & Tolich, M. B. (2012). *Planning ethically responsible research* (2nd ed., Applied Social Research Methods, Vol. 31). Thousand Oaks, CA: Sage.

U.S. Department of Health and Human Services, Office of Human Research Protections. (2017). *International compilation of human research standards.* Retrieved from https://www.hhs.gov/ohrp/international/compilation-human-research-standards/index.html

Part 7: Addressing Ethical Issues in Online Research

Buchanan, E. A., & Ess, C. (2008). Internet research ethics: The field and its critical issues. In K. E. Himma & H. T. Tavani (Eds.), *The handbook of information and computer ethics* (pp. 273–292). Hoboken, NJ: Wiley.

Harvard Catalyst Regulatory Foundations, Ethics, & Law Program. (n.d.) *The use of social media in recruitment to research: A guide for investigators and IRBs.* Retrieved from https://catalyst.harvard.edu/pdf/regulatory/Social_Media_Guidance.pdf

Hughes, J. (Ed.). (2012). *Sage internet research methods.* Thousand Oaks, CA: Sage.

Markham, A., & Buchanan, E. (2012). *Ethical decision-making and internet research: Recommendations from the AoIR Ethics Working Committee (Version 2.0).* Retrieved from http://aoir.org/reports/ethics2.pdf

Secretary's Advisory Committee on Human Research Protections. (2013). *Considerations and recommendations concerning internet research and human subjects research regulations, with revisions.* Final document, approved at SACHRP meeting March 12–13, 2013. Retrieved from http://www.hhs.gov/ohrp/sites/default/files/ohrp/sachrp/mtgings/2013%20March%20Mtg/internet_research.pdf

Sloan, L., & Quan-Haase, A. (Eds.). (2017). *The Sage handbook of social media research methods*. Thousand Oaks, CA: Sage.

Part 8: Negotiating the IRB Review Process

Corneli, A., & Borasky, D. (2015). Research ethics and working with institutional review boards. In Guest, G. S., & Namey, E. E. (Eds.), *Public health research methods* (pp. 69–100). Thousand Oaks, CA: Sage.

Both of these websites will have updated guidance on applying and interpreting federal regulations:
U.S. Department of Health and Human Services, Office of Human Research Protections. Retrieved from www.hhs.gov/ohrp
U.S. Department of Health and Human Services, Secretary's Advisory Committee on Human Research Protections. Retrieved from https://www.hhs.gov/ohrp/sachrp-committee/index.html

Consult your IRB's website for specific institutional requirements.

Part 9: Understanding Ethical Responsibilities of Data Use

NIH Data Sharing Policy. Retrieved from https://grants.nih.gov/grants/policy/data_sharing/
USAID's Open Data Policy. Retrieved from https://www.usaid.gov/data/frequently-asked-questions

Part 10: Handling Ethical Issues That Arise During Research Implementation

Given, L. M. (2016). *100 Questions (and answers) about qualitative research*. Thousand Oaks, CA: Sage.
Israel, M. (2014). *Research ethics and integrity for social scientists* (2nd ed.). Thousand Oaks, CA: Sage.
Mertens, D. M., & Ginsberg, P. E. (Eds.). (2009). *The handbook of social research ethics*. Thousand Oaks, CA: Sage.
Miller, T., Birch, M., Mauthner, M., & Jessop, J. (Eds.). (2012). *Ethics in qualitative research* (2nd ed.). Thousand Oaks, CA: Sage.
Morgan, D. L. (1997) *The focus group guidebook* (Focus Group Kit). Thousand Oaks, CA: Sage.

Index

Academic credit, for
   participation, 65–66
Adolescents, 100. *See also* Children
Age of majority, 100
Amendments, 160–161
American Anthropological
   Association, 14
American Educational Research
   Association, 14, 117
American Psychological Association,
   14, 117
American Sociological
   Association, 14
Anonymity, 37–38, 96
Appelbaum, P. S., 90
Assent, informed, 100–101
Authority. *See* Power
Autonomy, 50, 68, 89, 102, 118, 126.
   See also Respect for persons

Back-translation, 87
Belmont Report, 5, 6, 50, 68, 81, 93–94
Benefits of research, 5, 6, 25–26
   access to, 53
   balancing with risk, 27, 106
   misconceptions about, 28–29
   perception of, 27
   resources on, 191
Biospecimens, 78–79, 146–147
Broad consent, 96, 97
Burdens of research, 5

Certificate of Confidentiality
   (CoC), 46, 116
Chat rooms, 139
Children, 50, 52, 59–60
   informed assent, 100–101
   mature minor, 99
   parental permission and,
      52, 59–60, 66, 98, 100
   wards of the state, 60
Codes of ethics, 14, 117

Coercion, 11, 51, 82, 93
   prisoners and, 54–56
   of students, 66
Cognitive impairment,
   63–64, 89–90
Communities, defined,
   121–122, 124
Communities, disenfranchised, 124
Community, benefits for, 26
Community-based participatory
   research (CBPR), 123
Community engagement, 123–125
Compensation, 110–112.
   See also Incentives
Comprehension, 52, 91–92
   of consent forms, 80, 90
   of information, 81–82
   online research and, 138
Confidentiality, 22–23, 79
   after data collection, 168
   Certificate of Confidentiality (CoC),
      46, 116
   of consent forms, 84
   data sharing and, 175–176
   defined, 34
   de-identification, 21, 35–36,
      96, 168, 171
   in focus group discussions, 113
   maintaining, 41
   online research and, 133, 136
   in prison setting, 55–56
   recording and, 113
   resources on, 191–192
   secondary data analysis and, 96
   trauma victims and, 62
Conflicts of interest, 145
Consent, broad, 96, 97
Consent, implied, 73, 137
Consent, informed.
   See Informed consent
Consent, verbal, 74–75, 85
Consent forms, 71, 74

anonymity and, 38
comprehension of, 80, 90
confidentiality of, 84
easy-to-read, 80
information in, 77–79
storage of, 84
Continuing review, 152, 162–163
Control groups, 119–120
Covert observational research, 116
Cultural competence, 126–127

Data
confidentiality after
collection, 168
confidentiality of, 22–23
de-identification of, 21,
35–36, 96, 168, 171
destruction of, 171–172
falsifying, 11
loss of hard copies, 186
protection of, 34. See also
Confidentiality
retention of, 169
secondary data analysis, 96–97
Data collection
anonymity and, 37–38
online research, 133–134
privacy and, 34, 41
risk and, 30
Data sharing, 36, 175–176
mandatory, 44–45
resources on, 195
Data storage, 36, 42–43, 62
Debriefing, 14, 118
Deception, 11, 12–13, 14, 117–118
Decision-making capacity,
63–64, 83
Declaration of Helsinki, 6
Defined communities, 121–122, 124
De-identification of data, 21,
35–36, 96, 168, 171
Designing research, 37, 193–194
Developmental disability, 63, 89–90
Disenfranchised communities, 124
DuBois, J. M., 51

Education records, 47
Eligibility, 106
Ethics, defined, 2

Ethics training, 157
Exclusion criteria, 57, 106
Exempt research, 145, 147,
149–150, 166
Expedited review, 151, 152
Exploitation, 13
prisoners and, 54–56
of students, 65
vulnerability to, 50. See also
Vulnerable participants

Family Educational Rights and Privacy
Act (FERPA), 38, 47
Federal research regulations
(Code of Federal Regulations,
or CFR), 7, 155, 189
Fetuses, 50, 57
Financial incentives, 78, 93–94, 110–112
Focus group discussions, 113–114
Focus group transcripts, 177
Full board review, 152

Goffman, A., 13
Golden Rule, 2
Good, K., 13
Grisso, T., 90
Group membership, 121

Harm, 11, 12–13, 17
dignitary harm, 21
economic harm, 20
group-level harm, 20
legal harm, 21
minimizing, 30–31
participant threats of, 44–45,
46, 185
potential, 22. See also Risk
psychological harm, 20, 30–31
sharing information about, 44–45
social harm, 21, 61
vulnerability to, 50. See also
Vulnerable participants
See also Risk
Havasupai tribe, 121–122
Health Insurance Portability and
Accountability Act (HIPAA), 35, 38,
47, 108, 169
Human subjects
defined, 146

need for, 4
See also Participants
Humphreys, Laud, 12

Identifiers, 38, 78–79, 168
    collecting, 42
    destruction of, 43
    and destruction of data, 171
    See also Confidentiality;
        De-identification of data;
        Re-identification of data
Illegal activities, 13, 17, 50, 51,
    74–75, 116
Impartial witnesses, 85–86
Implied consent, 73, 137
Incentives, 66, 78, 93–94, 110–112
Inclusion criteria, 106
Information, in consent
    forms, 77–79
Information disclosure, 76, 81
Informed assent, 100–101
Informed consent, 11, 17, 47
    age of majority, 100
    children and, 83
    cognitive impairment and,
        63–64, 89–90
    comprehension of, 80, 81–82, 91–92
    consent forms, 71
    decision-making capacity and, 83
    defined, 68
    exemption from, 72
    information in, 77–79
    in international research,
        102–104
    language and, 87–88
    in observational research, 116
    obtaining, 80–81
    online research and, 133, 136,
        137–138
    parental permission, 52, 59–60, 66,
        98, 100
    process for, 69–70
    reading ability and, 85–86
    resources on, 193
    retention of records of, 170
    screening before receiving, 95
    for secondary data analysis, 96–97
    verbal, 74–75, 85
    voluntariness and, 93–94

waiver of, 72–73
written, 74
See also Consent forms
Informed consent process, 125, 126
Institutional policies, for IRBs, 155
Institutional review board (IRB),
    7, 11, 15–16
    appeals process, 159
    composition of, 144–145
    continuing review, 152, 162–163
    defined, 144
    determining need for review, 146–147
    expedited review, 151, 152
    full board review, 152
    institutional policies, 155
    materials to submit to, 153–154
    periodic review, 148
    program evaluation and, 165–166
    publication without approval
        from, 174
    resources on, 195
    responding to review, 158–159
    review process, 155
    single IRB, use of, for multisite
        studies, 148
    student projects and, 164
    submitting amendments, 160–161
International research, 15, 102–104, 128
    informed consent in, 102–104
    IRBs and, 148
Internet research. *See* Online research
IRB (institutional review board).
        See Institutional review board

Jonas, Hans, 4
Justice, 5, 6, 106

Kipnis, K., 51

Language, 126–127
    informed consent and, 87–88
Legally authorized representative, 89
Literacy, 52, 85–86

*MacArthur Competence Assessment Tool
    for Clinical Research*, 90
Mandatory reporting, 21, 44–45, 62
Mature minor, 99
Medical records, 47

Member checking, 177
Milgram, Stanley, 12, 117
Milgram Obedience Study, 12
Minor, mature, 99
Minors, 100. See also Children
Mobile phone apps, for
    online research, 134

National Commission for the Protection
    of Human Subjects of Biomedical
    and Behavioral Research, 6
National Institutes of Health
    (NIH), 46, 169, 175
National Science Foundation (NSF), 169
Neonates, 50, 57
Nixon, Richard, 6
Noncompliance, consequences of, 9
Nuremberg Code, 6

Observational research, 115–116
Office of Human Research Protections
    (OHRP), 7, 128, 151
Online groups, 139
Online research, 130
    comprehension and, 138
    confidentiality and, 133, 136
    data collection, 133–134
    identifying as researcher and, 139–140
    informed consent and, 133,
        136, 137–138
    institutional guidelines, 130
    online survey applications, 133
    privacy and, 133, 135–136
    privacy expectations and, 135
    recruitment for, 131–132
    resources on, 194–195
    verifying eligibility, 141
Online surveys, 133

Parental permission, 52, 59–60,
    66, 98, 100
Participant advocate, 52
Participant observations, 115–116
Participants
    preventing identification of, 41. See
        also Confidentiality;
        De-identification of data;
        Identifiers
    recruiting, 17. See also Recruitment

sharing results with, 179
sharing transcripts with, 177–178
threats to harm self/others,
    44–45, 46, 185
Participants, vulnerable. See
    Vulnerable participants
Participation, 7
    difficulty refusing, 11
    trust and, 10
Participatory action research (PAR), 123
Partner organizations, 108
Payment, 110–112
Personal information, 20. See also
    Confidentiality; Privacy
Post-traumatic stress disorder (PTSD), 62
Power, 51, 65
    prisoners and, 54–56
    recruitment and, 109
Pregnant women, 50, 57–58
Pretesting, 156
Prison, privacy/confidentiality in, 55–56
Prisoners, 50, 52, 54–56
    IRB and, 145
Privacy, 17, 20, 22
    data collection and, 34, 41
    defined, 34
    in focus group discussions, 113
    maintaining, 41
    observations and, 115
    online research and, 133, 135–136
    in prison setting, 55–56
    protection of, 41
    recruitment and, 107–109
    resources on, 191–192
    See also Confidentiality
Privacy expectations, 135
Privacy laws, 47
Private information, 39–40
Professional associations, resources
    from, 189
Program evaluation, 165
Protocol, changes to, 182–183
Protocol violations, 182–183
Publication
    ethical obligations, 173
    IRB approval and, 166
    without informed consent, 174
    without IRB approval, 174
Public information, 39–40

Randomized controlled trials (RCT), 119–120
Reading ability, 52, 85–86
Recruitment, 17, 107–109, 131–132
Redaction, in transcripts, 114
Re-identification of data, 35, 43, 175
Reimbursement for research participation, 110–112
Research, definition of, 146
Research ethics, defined, 2
Research ethics boards (REBs), 15. *See also* Institutional review board (IRB)
Resources
  on benefits, 191
  on confidentiality, 191–192
  on data sharing, 195
  on informed consent, 193
  on IRB, 195
  on online research, 194–195
  on privacy, 191–192
  from professional associations, 189
  on risks, 191
  on vulnerable participants, 192–193
Respect for persons, 5, 6, 13, 17. *See also* Autonomy
Responsibility, for ethics, 15
Results, sharing with participants, 179
Retention of data, 169
Retraumatization, 61
Rights, of participants, 17
Risk, 5
  assessing, 20
  balancing with benefits, 27, 106
  community engagement and, 125
  of daily living, 24
  data collection and, 30
  defined, 20
  economic risk, 22
  in focus group discussions, 113–114
  group-level risk, 21, 121
  identifying, 22
  legal risk, 22
  likelihood of, 23
  magnitude of, 23
  minimal risk, 20, 24
  minimizing, 23
  misconceptions about, 28–29
  perception of, 27

psychological risk, 22
resources on, 191
social risk, 22
unreasonable, 11
See also Harm
Risk-benefit balance, 106

Screening questions, 95
Secondary data analysis, 96–97
Self-care, 62
Services, 28
Sharing, of data, 175–176
Snowballing, 109
Stanford Prison Study, 13
Stigmatized behavior, 51
Storage
  of consent forms, 84
  of data, 36, 42–43, 62
Student projects, 164
Students, 65–66
Study design, anonymity and, 37
Subjects, human. *See* Human subjects; Participants
Surrogate decision maker, 52, 64

Teachers, research by, 65–66
Tearoom Trade Study, 12–13
Therapeutic misconception, 28, 62
Training, ethical, 157
Transcriptionist, 187
Transcripts
  omitting names from, 187
  sharing with participants, 177–178
Translation, 87–88, 103
Trauma victims, 61–62
Trust, public, 9–10
Tuskegee Syphilis Study, 6

Understanding, 91–92. *See also* Comprehension
Undue influence, 93–94
Unethical research, examples of, 11–12
United States Agency for International Development (USAID), 175
U.S. Department of Health and Human Services (HHS), 46

Verbal consent, 74–75, 85
Voluntariness, 72, 78, 80, 82, 93–94

Vulnerable participants, 50–53
  children, 59–60
  cognitive impairment, 63–64
  decision-making capacity, 63–64
  pregnant women, 57–58
  prisoners, 54–56
  resources on, 192–193
  trauma victims, 61–62

Waiver of informed
  consent, 74–75
Wards of the state, 60
Women, pregnant,
  50, 57–58
World Medical Association, 6

Zimbardo, Philip, 13